Sumerians

A Captivating Guide to Ancient Sumerian History, Sumerian Mythology and the Mesopotamian Empire of the Sumer Civilization

© **Copyright 2018**

All rights Reserved. No part of this book may be reproduced in any form without permission in writing from the author. Reviewers may quote brief passages in reviews.

Disclaimer: No part of this publication may be reproduced or transmitted in any form or by any means, mechanical or electronic, including photocopying or recording, or by any information storage and retrieval system, or transmitted by email without permission in writing from the publisher.

While all attempts have been made to verify the information provided in this publication, neither the author nor the publisher assumes any responsibility for errors, omissions or contrary interpretations of the subject matter herein.

This book is for entertainment purposes only. The views expressed are those of the author alone, and should not be taken as expert instruction or commands. The reader is responsible for his or her own actions.

Adherence to all applicable laws and regulations, including international, federal, state and local laws governing professional licensing, business practices, advertising and all other aspects of doing business in the US, Canada, UK or any other jurisdiction is the sole responsibility of the purchaser or reader.

Neither the author nor the publisher assumes any responsibility or liability whatsoever on the behalf of the purchaser or reader of these materials. Any perceived slight of any individual or organization is purely unintentional.

Free Bonus from Captivating History (Available for a Limited time)

Hi History Lovers!

Now you have a chance to join our exclusive history list so you can get your first history ebook for free as well as discounts and a potential to get more history books for free! Simply visit the link below to join.

Captivatinghistory.com/ebook

Also, make sure to follow us on:

Twitter: @Captivhistory

Facebook: Captivating History:@captivatinghistory

Contents

FREE BONUS FROM CAPTIVATING HISTORY (AVAILABLE FOR A LIMITED TIME) 5

AN INTRODUCTION TO ANCIENT SUMERIANS 1

CHAPTER 1 4

THE ANCIENT SUMERIANS IN A NUTSHELL: WHO WERE THEY? WHERE DID THEY LIVE? WHERE DID THEY COME FROM? THE TIMELINE OF THE SUMERIAN CIVILIZATION; POTENTIAL GENETIC MAKE-UP OF THE SUMERIANS 4

    Who Were the Sumerians? 5
    Where Did the Sumerians Live? 5
    Where Did Sumerians Come From? 6
    The Timeline of the Sumerian Civilization 7
    Potential Genetic Make-up of the Sumerians 9
    Conclusion 9

CHAPTER 2 11

THE SOCIAL STRUCTURE OF ANCIENT SUMERIANS: RULERS, PRIESTS, PRIVILEGED CLASSES, ORDINARY PEOPLE, SLAVES; GENDER DIFFERENCES; CHILDREN 11

    The Ensi 12
    The Assembly 12
    Priests 13
    Sumerian Social Classes and Their Privileges 14
    Men and Women of Sumer 16
    Children of Sumer 17
    Conclusion 17

CHAPTER 3 19

THE RELIGION AND MYTHOLOGY OF ANCIENT SUMERIANS: COSMOLOGY, MAJOR AND MINOR GODS, RITUALS, MYTHS; MISCONCEPTIONS AND PSEUDOSCIENTIFIC EXPLANATIONS 19

    The Cosmology of Sumerians 20
    The Sumerian Pantheon 21

HEAVEN AND THE UNDERWORLD 24
RELIGIOUS RITUALS AND PRACTICES.. 25
SUMERIAN MYTHS 26
MISCONCEPTIONS AND MODERN PSEUDOSCIENCE................................... 28

CHAPTER 4 29

THE SUMERIAN KINGDOMS CHRONOLOGY: THE LIST OF CITY-STATES, DYNASTIES, AND PROMINENT RULERS 29

SUMERIAN CITY-STATES 30
   Eridu.. *31*
   Uruk... *32*
   Ur *33*
   Lagash *34*
   Nippur.. *35*
   Larsa.. *36*
   Kish.. *37*
   Umma *37*
   Shuruppak... *38*
   Bad-tibira *38*
   Isin... *39*
   Other Cities *39*
SUMERIAN DYNASTIES.. 41
   The Early Dynastic Period – Antediluvians, City-state rulers................... *42*
   The Akkadian Period, or the Sargonic Era.. *45*
   The Gutian Period.. *46*
   The Third Dynasty of Ur, or the Sumerian Renaissance *46*
   The Isin-Larsa Period... *47*
NOTABLE RULERS OF SUMER... 48
   Enmebaragesi of Kish... *48*
   Enmerkar of Uruk.. *48*
   Lugalbanda of Uruk *48*
   Gilgamesh of Uruk *49*
   Meshanepada of Ur *49*
   Eannatum of Lagash... *49*
   Urukagina of Lagash... *50*
   Lugal-Anne-Mundu of Adab *51*
   Kug-Bau of Kish *51*
   Ur-Zababa of Kish... *51*
   Lugal-Zage-Si... *51*
   Sargon of Akkad *52*
   Gudea of Lagash.. *52*
   Utu-Hengal of Uruk... *53*
   Ur-Nammu of Ur *54*
   Shulgi of Ur *54*
   Ibbi-Sin of Ur.. *55*

    Ishbi-Erra of Isin......55
    Damiq-Ilishu of Isin......55
    Rim-Sin I of Larsa......55
  CONCLUSION......56

CHAPTER 5......57

THE EVERYDAY LIFE OF ANCIENT SUMERIANS: JOBS AND PROFESSIONS, TRAVEL, HOUSING, SOCIAL LIFE; PSYCHOLOGICAL AND ETHICAL MAKE-UP 57

  JOBS AND PROFESSIONS......58
  TRAVEL......61
  HOUSING......61
  SOCIAL LIFE......62
  PSYCHOLOGICAL AND ETHICAL MAKE-UP OF ANCIENT SUMERIANS......62
  CONCLUSION......64

CHAPTER 6......65

SUMERIAN INNOVATIONS: ARCHITECTURE AND TECHNOLOGY..65

  SUMERIAN ARCHITECTURE......65
    Houses......65
    Temples......66
    Ziggurats......67
    Palaces......68
    Outdoor Planning and Landscaping......69
  SUMERIAN TECHNOLOGY......70
  CONCLUSION......71

CHAPTER 7......72

SUMERIAN CULTURE: LITERATURE, ART, MUSIC 72

  LITERATURE......72
  ART......74
  MUSIC......77
  CONCLUSION......79

SUMERIAN "FOREIGN POLICY": RELATIONS WITH OTHER NATIONS......81

  LANDS WITH UNKNOWN OR UNCONFIRMED LOCATIONS......81
  RELATIONS WITH THE OTHER PEOPLES......83
    Gutians and Hurrians......83
    The Semites of Mesopotamia......84
  CONCLUSION......85

SUMERIANS......86

CONCLUSION 86
BIBLIOGRAPHY AND REFERENCES 114
NOTES ON IMAGES 116

An Introduction to Ancient Sumerians

Ancient history is always a fascinating subject. For a layman, it stands as a romantic look of our ancestors - how "times were different" and how people lived on without the commodities modern man has today. For a historian worth their salt, the ancient people are an endless source of information, good indicators of how we're moving along as a collective humanity, though they captivate on the micro level as well from the individual to the state or country itself. In short, learning from this past equips us to function better in the future, and occasionally chuckle when we find a relatable datum that speaks to us personally.

And on the note of speaking to us personally, each region has a fascination with its own history, and the history of the people immediately surrounding it. Europeans continue to learn from Ancient Greeks and Romans, paying close attention to other cultures that surrounded them such as Illyrians, Thracians, Celts, etc. Africans look to Egypt, Ethiopia, Nubia, and other massive kingdoms and empires that dominated the continent. Asians have a massive number of cultural clusters to research, such as Ancient China and the cultures on the Indian Subcontinent. The Americas and Australia, while themselves descendants from Europeans, look to the cultures of their native peoples, thus we learn more about Aztecs, Mayans, Incas, the

Aboriginal people of Australia, the Native American tribes of North America, and so on.

However, all of this had to have started somewhere. And what is often known as the 'cradle of civilization' happens to be in Asia Minor, or the Middle East as it is now socio-politically better known. This is the area between the large rivers known as Tigris and Euphrates, and because of this location it bears the name Mesopotamia, "land between the rivers." But Mesopotamia itself had numerous cultures: Persians, Syrians, Assyrians, Amorites, Elamites, Babylonians, Hittites, Hurrians, and, later on, Romans and various Muslim sects and subgroups. Still, one culture had to be the first, and that would be the Ancient Sumerians.

The sheer importance of Sumerian culture in regards to world culture as a whole is impossible to overstate. This civilization is single-handedly responsible for some of the most major innovations in nearly every field relevant to maintaining a civilized society - this includes religion, lawmaking, architecture, schooling, art, literature, and even entertainment. Naturally, most of what we see as negative aspects of society were established in Ancient Sumer as well. There wasn't an aspect of Sumerian life that wasn't plagued with corruption or devastation of one form or another. In other words, the Sumerians gave us both the sublimeness of faith and the rigidness of religious thought coupled with a desire for political supremacy. They gave us both the benevolent, caring monarchs and cruel, punishing tyrants; the educated child and the spoiled brat; the hard-working agrarian and the drunken reveler; and the epic empires as well as the pathetic remnants of them. The Sumerians did it all, and they did it first.

Sadly, their culture is long gone. And as is often the case with ancient cultures, as interesting as they may be to a reader or a curious pair of eyes, they tend not to be relatable because of the massive time gap between them and us, which in this case spans no less than 7,000 years, at least. But this book will give you the gist of what Sumerians were like. You will learn about the people themselves, how they organized their society, what they believed and how they believed in it, what their now famous city-states were like and who ruled over them, how they went about their everyday lives, what they invented or reinvented that we still utilize today, how their culture developed throughout the millennia, and how they interacted with other peoples surrounding them. And the reason the Sumerians in particular should matter to you, as both a reader and a proponent of your current culture, is a simple one - being the first, the Sumerians are not just Asia-specific; they are part of our common heritage, and as such are likely our direct cultural and civilizational ancestors. And the old adage of treating elders with respect matters here as well, especially if said elders can return that respect tenfold with invaluable information and fascinating facts.

Chapter 1

The Ancient Sumerians In a Nutshell: Who Were They? Where Did They Live? Where Did They Come From? The Timeline of the Sumerian Civilization; Potential Genetic Make-up of the Sumerians

The absolute majority of scholars around the world agree that the Ancient Sumerians were the earliest developed civilization in our recorded history. This doesn't mean that they are the oldest recorded humanoid beings on our planet - recent discoveries in Greece and Bulgaria give us some idea of the earliest human, earlier even than Lucy, who was located in Africa. It doesn't even necessarily mean that their culture was the first to fashion simple tools from stone, iron, or bronze. However, they are the culture that gave us a lot of firsts: the first kingdom, and then empire, the first city-states, the first democracy, the first autocracy; they pioneered writing, schooling, organized religion, lawmaking, art, and literature. Yes, the Sumerians were the first in many an area of expertise.

However, we should first discuss the people themselves. We will cover where they lived, their potential place of origin before Ancient Mesopotamia, how their civilization came to be, and how it developed throughout the ages. We will also try and see what their potential genetic make-up was when compared to other people living in the area.

Who Were the Sumerians?

The Sumerians were a civilization that would go on to influence the entirety of the Ancient Middle East, and their accomplishments and innovations echo in diverse ancient cultures such as Egypt, Greece, Rome, Ethiopia, and more. From a practical, mundane standpoint, they were a highly religious, agricultural society that put great emphasis on art, culture, and the written word. As is the case with all cultures, they developed from simpler hunter-gatherer societies, based on the Bronze age sites scattered about the area that comprised Ancient Sumer. They were an innovative, inventive, imaginative people and, interestingly enough, had parallels with even modern-day societies in both positive and negative aspects of their daily lives. All of this will be covered in more detail in further chapters.

Where Did the Sumerians Live?

The area where the earliest civilization lived took up the territory of Southern Mesopotamia, in parts of modern Iraq and Kuwait. It is nestled between two important rivers for the region, the Tigris and the Euphrates, as well as the Persian Gulf to the southeast. Their earliest "countries" were numerous city-states that, depending on the time period, either dominated the region, were enslaved by other cities or even other peoples, or acted independently. We will go into more detail on these cities when we cover the dynasties and rulers of Ancient Sumer.

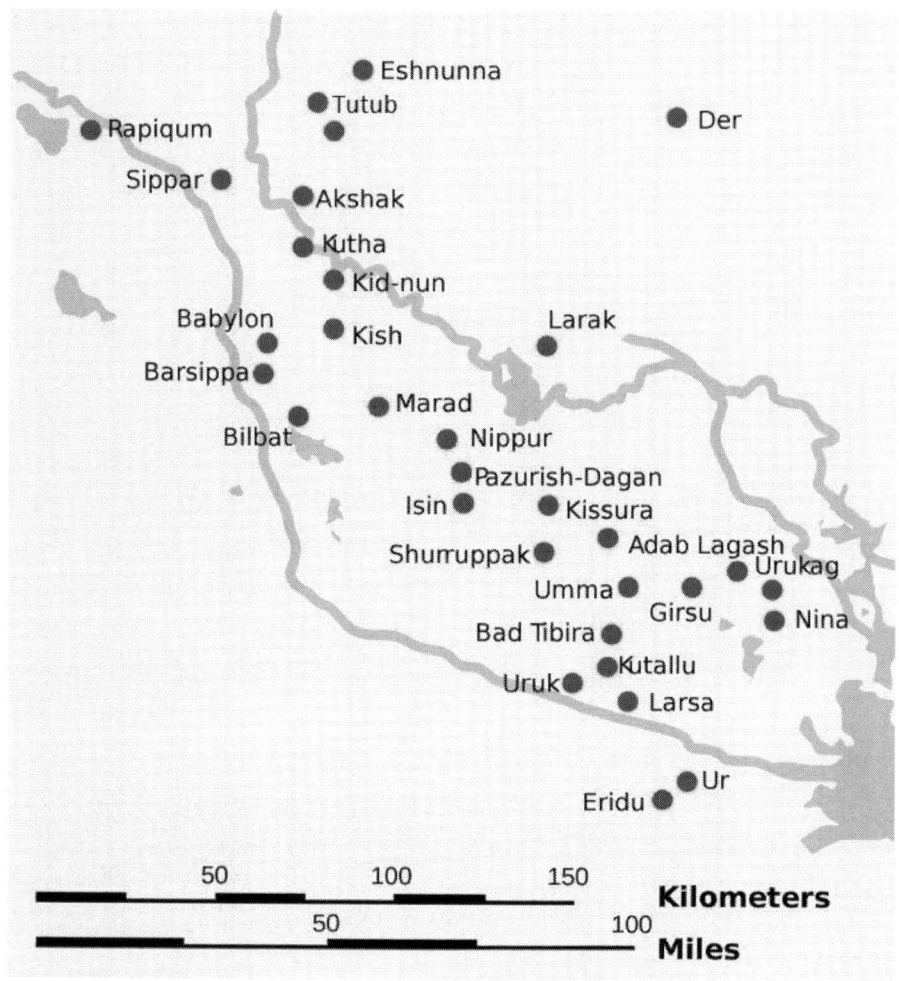

Map of Sumerian and Elamite cities. [i] *Original image by Phirosiberia.*

Where Did Sumerians Come From?

This is an interesting topic that gets touched upon from time to time but not to any major extent. Normally the supposition is that the Sumerians came from either modern-day India or from the west of the two rivers. However, an interesting new archeological development may place them at a different place altogether. Studying several independent factors, such as the religious and cultural importance of lapis lazuli for the Sumerians, the archeological sites where there were frequent excavations of this stone at a time before the Sumerians settled Southern Mesopotamia, and studies of biogeographical DNA of ancient peoples in the Middle East, plausibly places the Sumerians' ancestors in Neolithic and Bronze Age sites such as Gonur Tepe and Anau in modern-day Turkmenistan. If this hypothesis turns out to be true, it would mean that the earliest settlers of Sumer came there after a major drought struck their place of residence close to the lapis lazuli mines. However, despite leaving, they kept their culture and myths which relied heavily on lapis lazuli usage and excavation.

The Timeline of the Sumerian Civilization

Sumerian scholars have, in the past century and a half at least, managed to piece together a plausible timeline of Ancient Mesopotamia in terms of human settlements and early cultures. The earliest period with permanent towns in the region is called the Ubaid period, named after a small uncovered settlement Tell al-'Ubaid near ancient Ur. This period roughly starts circa 6500 BC and ends around 4100 BC. It encompasses the earliest human culture in the region that predates "modern" Sumerians, and is marked by several major events. The city of Eridu, the oldest Sumerian settlement based on available data, was founded in 5400 BC, and four centuries later, the Ubaid people settled Godin Tepe. At the same time, we get early signs of burials, and the Sumerian culture officially starts blooming into existence.

What follows is the Uruk Period. Five centuries after the Ubaid people settled the Sumerian lands, the city of Uruk was founded, and they built their first temple. The Uruk Period lasts 1200 years, circa 4100-2900 BC. During this period, writing was in full swing in Uruk. It is estimated that it was invented around 3,600 BC with the first religious texts a century later, and it was in frequent use by 3,200 BC.

Right after that follows the Early Dynastic period. It spans from 2900 BC to 2334 BC. It is within this period that we find royal graves in the city of Ur. King Eannatum ruled over the city of Lagash in about 2500 BC, thus forming the First Dynasty of this city. This begins the first recorded empire in Sumer. At this time, non-religious literature such as myths and poetry was becoming a prominent feature in the city-states, especially in Lagash. About a century later, around 2350 BC, their king Urukagina wrote the first code of law; this would become a basis for all future law codes in the immediate region.

In 2334 BC, Sargon of Akkad took over most of Sumerian lands, making him one of the first emperors of the Middle East with a multiethnic, expansive empire. The reign of his dynasty lasted until about 2218 BC, when the Gutian Period begins in Sumer. The nomadic Gutians took control of the Sumerian lands, replacing the Akkadian rulers that succeeded Sargon. A little over half a century after the Gutian conquest, the first tablets of the Epic of Gilgamesh were being written. Utu-Hegal tookcontrol of Sumer—and certain Akkadian cities—back from the Gutians at around 2055 BC, and he is succeeded by Ur-Nammu in 2048 BC. This is the period when the Third Dynasty of Ur reigned over Sumer, yet it includes more than just this dynasty.

This period started with the reign of Ur-Nammu and ended a little after 1750 BC, with the invasion of Elamites and the Amorites migrating to the area. There were significant changes during this era, known as the Sumerian Renaissance. Ur-Nammu's successor, King Shulgi, built the so-called Great Wall of Uruk at around 2038 BC, which stood fast throughout the period. In the period mid-1900 BC the last vestige of the Third Dynasty of Ur ends with Ibi-Sin, at around 1940 BC. The final Sumerian, or rather Akkadian, dynasty to reign over what was left of their vast empire was the Dynasty of Isin. The empire itself fell under post-Hammurabi Babylon at around 1750 BC, which is marked as the end of the Sumerian civilization altogether. The Babylonian ruler Hammurabi had codified his famous Code some twenty-two years earlier, based on earlier Sumerian codes.

Naturally, most of these dates are estimates at best. The Sumerian chronology is somewhat difficult to read (there will be more info on this in the Sumerian rulers' section) because of how the cuneiform sources are written. Nevertheless, most of the prominent events can be dated with some accuracy based on peripheral evidence, so we can speak about the Sumerian rise to prominence and decline with a good degree of certainty.

Potential Genetic Make-up of the Sumerians

This particular topic obviously didn't come up a whole lot in the early days of Mesopotamian studies. But with the advent of DNA research, the question of genetic origins of Ancient Sumerians was raised once more. An extensive survey of Y-chromosome and mtDNA variation among the Marsh Arabs of Iraq heavily implies that they are direct descendants of Sumerians. This also brought about a separate topic, that of whether or not the Sumerians were autochthonous or of Indian or South Asian ancestry. Based on the findings, the Marsh Arabs, who've been in the area of Southern Mesopotamia for generations, share more common ancestry with the Assyrians and the Iraqis than with any other people group (the test groups involved Indians, Mediterranean Europeans, Israeli Druze, Palestinians, the Khuzestani Arabs, Africans, Pacific Asians and more). This implied that the ancestors of the Marsh Arabs did not move from different areas but were autochthonous for at least as long as the Sumerians were present. Naturally, this doesn't go against the hypothesis that the Sumerians originated from the modern-day Turkmenistan region, but rather explains away the potential genetic and even physical make-up of the earliest civilization.

Conclusion

If you merely look at the timeline presented above, you'll see that Sumerian life and culture spans no less than four and a half millennia. That's an enormous time span that presents a real treasure trove of archeological and historical gems. If we take into account their possible origins, coupled with how they moved and settled in a lower, more arable region, we can accurately draw a picture of even this ancient culture's more ancient past. We can see first-hand how migrations and climate change affected the earliest civilization, how they were responsible for their way of life, their religious beliefs, as well as their possible aspirations and ambitions. In the upcoming chapters, we will take a closer, more detailed, look at the Sumerians' way of life, on every level of society. Naturally, we will cover their technological and cultural advances and how they influenced the cultures around them, bleeding into numerous diverse lands across the known globe in ancient times.

Chapter 2

The Social Structure of Ancient Sumerians: Rulers, Priests, Privileged Classes, Ordinary People, Slaves; Gender Differences; Children

For the longest time, many scholars agreed that the ancient Sumerians were a predominantly autocratic, authoritarian society. In other words, they were supposedly more in line with other ancient cultures such as Egypt, China, and even their direct "descendants" the Babylonians. However, this is not the case, or at least not for the entirety of the existence of Sumerians. From their earliest days, the Sumerian city-states actually enjoyed a level of democracy not unlike the one we have today in the Western world. Most major government positions were elected rather than hereditary, and a council made important decisions regarding critical state matters. It was only during increasing warfare between the city states, as well as clashes with the barbaric tribes from both the East and the West of Sumer, that the need for a single ruler arose, and this was when the king or Lugal— "big man" in Sumerian—would take control.

The Ensi

In the beginning, every city state had a ruler, called an Ensi. In the earlier periods of Sumer, an Ensi would merely act as an elected "governor" of the city, a title he would maintain only until the next one got elected. He was seen as an elected peer among peers and wasn't the sole person deciding upon important city matters. In fact, there's scarce evidence that there was even need of Ensis during important court proceedings. During the Early Dynastic Period, an Ensi would represent the patron god of the city. However, in later periods, an Ensi would be subordinate to a Lugal, but this distinction is still up for debate even today. Many powerful rulers would later take up Ensi as their title rather than Lugal. During the last Sumerian dynasty to rule over these lands, the Third Dynasty of Ur, the title of Ensi was almost entirely relegated to local city governors second only to a Lugal. Their positions remained hereditary but only if they were to the Lugal's liking.

The Assembly

As stated earlier, the Ensi was initially not the supreme ruler of the city-state in Ancient Sumer. Most major decisions were deliberated on by a bicameral assembly. This assembly consisted of two houses, the Upper and the Lower houses. The Upper house consisted of "elders," mainly members of nobility and priestly classes. The Lower house, consequently, most likely consisted of commoners, mainly men of less noble or even commoner background.

The assembly would deliberate mainly on everyday state matters, such as food production, trade, disaster relief, foreign affairs, legal disputes, and so on. During times of war, they would elect a single military commander for the duration of the conflict, which inevitably led to the birth of the Lugal. What's interesting to note is that during the course of Sumerian civilization, based on thousands of archived correspondence and official documents of the time, this top structure of the Sumerian city state would show the same interchanging periods of prosperity and corruption, not unlike many of our modern countries. In this regard, Sumer is the birthplace of both hereditary monarchy, liberal(ish) democracy, and, as we will see in the section on Sumerian rulers such as Urukagina, government corruption.

Priests

An Ensi would also act as a head priest of the temple belonging to the city state's patron god, while his wife would be the head priestess for the city's patron goddess. In later years, it was not uncommon for an Ensi to declare himself a god, thus making the temple personnel take care of him directly. Each temple would have two chief administrators, the En and the Sanga. While there might be an overlap between an En and an Ensi (and Lugal, for that matter), from what we know, an En oversaw the duties of all present priests and priestesses in the temple. Each priest or priestess had a different duty, largely related to hymn writing and music composing, food preparation and feeding of "gods," clothing them, etc. Other priests would perform religious duties directly to the people of the city. Not uncommon was the priests' performing of exorcisms, purifications, medical treatments, prayer, and education. The Sanga, on the other hand, handled the business end of the temple. This meant dealing with trade, providing jobs to the city's inhabitants, overseeing at times thousands of jobs around the temple, and much more. While the En oversaw the priests directly, the Sanga oversaw the weavers, chefs, housekeepers, scribes, butchers, guards, accountants, artisans, messengers, and seamstresses. In short, the everyday workers not belonging to a priestly class.

Contrary to what earlier scholars believed, the temple did not "own" all of the land in a city state. In fact, only the temple grounds were under direct temple ownership. This land, unlike the land owned by private citizens outside of the temple, could not be sold, bought, or its ownership passed around in any manner. In short, it belonged to the main god of the city, i.e., to the priests currently occupying it. There will be more word on the temple grounds themselves in a later chapter.

The priests were part of the nobility in Ancient Sumer. Considering how important their role was in maintaining spirituality in Sumerian cities, this is hardly a surprise. As nobles, they participated in matters concerning the city state at the assembly (as part of the Upper house), were involved with Ensi election, and could own private land. Normally this would be land directly adjacent to, or even belonging to, the main temple. Due to their wealth, reputation, and position, most priests were literate and well-educated, often serving as scribes. They served as the original doctors and dentists of Ancient Sumerians, providing medical aid parallel to spiritual care. Other skills they would excel at included music and art, largely used for liturgical or ceremonial purposes.

In order to become a priest or a priestess, a young man or woman had to come from a noble family, and be of healthy body and mind. Celibacy was required with priestesses, though they could act as stepmothers to their husbands' children. Priestly training was grueling and difficult, but it yielded great privilege and knowledge.

Sumerian Social Classes and Their Privileges

Based on extensive research of both early and late Sumerian sources, we can divide up the Sumerian socioeconomic structure into four major groups. The first group were the nobles. This would include the Ensi and his spouse, the priests, local princes, and men of renown. As mentioned earlier, they most likely made up the Upper house of the city assembly. This class owned large areas of land, be it through private or family property. This included temple land as well.

The second group were the commoners. They were not as well-off as the nobility and could only own land as members of a family, not as individuals. Nevertheless, if there ever arose any dispute regarding land or even trade, they could participate either with the higher member of nobility or as a stand-in should he be absent. In terms of free citizenry, this would be the lowest class.

The third group were the so-called "clients," and they consisted of three other subgroups: well-to-do temple dependents, the temple personnel, and the dependents of nobles. The first and the second subgroup were known to possess small patches of temple land, though not permanently. Some members of these subgroups also got compensation in the form of food and wool rations. The last subgroup were most likely paid by their respective nobles in accordance to their work input.

The fourth major group were the slaves. As is the case with most ancient cultures, the Sumerians were no strangers to slavery. However, it was not nearly as rigorous as its later iterations in more powerful societies, like Syria, Persia, and even early European lands. In fact, a Sumerian slave retained some legal rights. For instance, a Sumerian slave was well-treated, largely because a Sumerian master would require a slave in fit condition to work. This doesn't mean that slaves didn't get severely punished or treated differently to other chattel during trade, however. A healthy slave would cost less than a donkey on the Sumerian market. And in terms of treatment, if a slave were to try escaping, they would be flogged and branded brutally by their owner.

A male slave in Sumer could engage in trade, and even borrow money to buy himself freedom. If, on the other hand, a slave were to marry a free citizen of any class, their children would qualify as free citizens as well. Becoming a slave, on the other hand, was unsurprisingly much easier. The most common way was enslaving members of non-Sumerian tribes or even Sumerians from neighboring city states during a war. A free citizen that failed to pay his debts or broke any severe law would also become a slave. Furthermore, parents had the legal right to sell their children into slavery if they faced hard financial times. Astoundingly, a man might turn over his entire family to creditors if he needed to repay his debt, but their term of slavery would not last longer than three years. The majority of slaves were men, considering their physical advantages to women, children and the elderly, and they were usually used mainly to do hard physical labor, primarily field work or construction.

Left: Male Worshipper of Tell Asmar; Right: Sumerian Woman.[ii] Original image by *Xuan Che and* Osama Shukir.

Men and Women of Sumer

During all of the Sumerian dynasties, men were normally treated better than women, although women enjoyed a plentitude of legal rights, like any commoner. They could hold property independently of men, for instance. In addition, they could engage in independent enterprise, doing business like any man would. And legally speaking, a woman could act as a viable witness just like a man would, unlike, for instance, the Islamic culture which would come to dominate this area many millennia later, where multiple women must serve as witness in a single man's stead. And while a woman could not be an Ensi, she could still hold a high position within the temple. In this respect, the Sumerians were somewhat progressive. However, a man could still divorce his wife on light grounds with zero repercussions and even marry a second wife if his first bore him no children.

Children of Sumer

When it comes to children, most laws that applied to any adult commoner applied to them: they could be sold off, bought, and freed as slaves, and as mentioned in the slavery section, a child born to a free man and a slave woman (or vice versa) would instantly become a free citizen. In terms of family, the children were under the absolute authority of their parents. This means that a parent could disinherit a child at any point in life. However, any land that a parent owned (outside of temple land, of course) was hereditary, meaning that children would get it upon the parents' death. But this was all just true legally speaking. In terms of their familial relationships, children were treated with utmost love and care by their parents. In fact, this is something that was in practice with both biological and adopted children. Adoption was a somewhat common practice in Ancient Sumer, and a non-biological child would have all the rights a direct blood descendant would have, as well as all of the limitations.

Conclusion

From what we know, the early Sumerians were pioneers in many socioeconomic fields. Their earliest social structures were democratic in nature, and only turned autocratic later on during the time of great conquests and natural disasters. The social classes in Sumer more or less reflect modern society, if we exclude slavery. But even slavery was lighter in nature to the cultures that came after Sumer, including their direct successors. We've also learned that the treatment of women and children was somewhat more progressive than in later cultures, with some important caveats, of course. An important bit to note is the ownership of private property, which will be touched upon in more detail in later chapters. This meant that the power structures were not originally as authoritarian as, for instance, during the time of Lugals, but rather that the most important institution in the city, the temple, operated within its own circle and that all land beyond it was owned by most of the other classes.

In addition, we can see the earliest forms of a parliamentary system in the form of the city assembly, and from its division into the Upper and Lower houses, we can conclude that matters of state were not just in the hands of nobility. It is endlessly interesting that both the democratic voting system and the autocratic reign of a single monarch stem from the same basic source and that both of these systems, in various forms, continued on existing in countless other cultures hence, all over the world and across many millennia.

Chapter 3

The Religion and Mythology of Ancient Sumerians: Cosmology, Major and Minor Gods, Rituals, Myths; Misconceptions and Pseudoscientific Explanations

Understanding this particular aspect of the Ancient Sumerians is of vital importance to world culture in general. And no, this is not a statement made lightly. Most of what we see in the ancient myths of Sumer either directly or partially corresponds to numerous world myths, the hierarchy and behavior of gods, the creation of man, the great flood, the giants, the creation myths, all of these were present in Sumerian mythology first. Now it's important to note that many modern scholars claim that other Near Eastern cultures didn't necessarily "borrow" these myths, or elements thereof, and reinterpret them as their own. Rather, the consensus is that all of them, Sumerians included, wrote their myths based on a common source.

Considering the lack of substantial data on this subject, due in part to the state of the available data (missing tablets, damaged tablets, entire sections that cannot as yet be translated or interpreted, etc.), most of what we know about Sumerian beliefs comes as a result of patching together pieces of information. It doesn't help that oftentimes a scribe from a Sumerian temple would be inconsistent with their work, as tablets were found describing the same event in the same temple, in the same period no less, vastly different. Nevertheless, enough has been found to at least provide a basic idea of what Ancient Sumerians believed and how they acted according to their religious duties.

The Cosmology of Sumerians

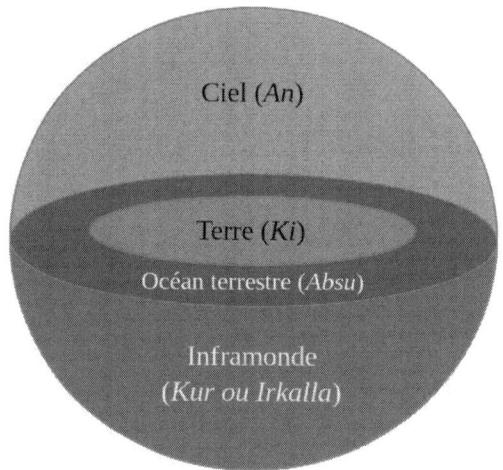

The Cosmology of Sumer.[iii]

If you were to have asked an Ancient Sumerian what their world looked like, they would have described it as a closed dome surrounded by a primordial, saltwater sea. Beneath what was the terrestrial earth, or Ma, lay a freshwater ocean, and it was called Apsu, or Abzu. The operating belief was that all fresh water—rivers, lakes, streams, rivulets—all came from this subterranean ocean. Directly below Abzu was the Sumerian underworld known as Kur. This was where the deceased ended up, be they humans or gods. The dome presented a heavenly firmament, where most of the gods dwelled and whose chief deity was An. In the beginning, the heaven and the earth, or rather the heavenly firmament and the terrestrial ocean, were essentially one being, called Anki, and they came out of the primordial waters known as the goddess Nammu. Between heaven and earth there was a substance called Lil, which could roughly be translated as "atmosphere" or "air." Nammu is important because she/it surrounded the entire known universe of Sumerians as an endless ocean. The universe itself would remain unmovable within Nammu.

The Sumerian Pantheon

A god, or dingir, was in the eyes of Sumerian people of faith an anthropomorphic being that boasted immense immortal powers, and was responsible for overseeing a particular aspect of the known universe. A minor contradiction exists in terms of the actions of these gods in the many written works of Ancient Sumerians—despite being powerful and immortal, they still required food and water, and they could be harmed, killed, sent to the underworld, severely punished, and so on. In fact, not even the chief deities were immune to this. This humanizing of Sumerian gods is an element that would pass over into other Near Eastern and Mediterranean religions and most likely stems from priests' attempts to explain away the universe through familiar means.

Analogous to the organization of the city-state, the Sumerian pantheon was also hierarchical in nature. Initially, the pantheon recognized seven major deities who "decreed the fates of man," with one serving as the king, and at least fifty minor deities known as "the great gods." By the time of the Third Dynasty of Ur, the number of deities went as high as 3600. The major seven gods were An, Enlil, Enki, Ninhursag (or Ki), Nanna-Sin, Utu, and Innana.

An was the progenitor of all gods. In fact, the term Annunaki, "children of An and Ki" or "princely seed," the name for the gods who decreed the fates of man, derives from him. Having come from the primordial waters Nammu, he copulated with the earth goddess Ki, producing children. They formed a single entity known as Anki, which would later be separated by their son Enlil. An was the chief deity of early Sumerians; however, his role shifted into obscurity as he gave way to Enlil in importance. His role was that of the god who contains the entire universe, and who is the supreme authority of all other gods and men.

Enlil, originally the god of wind, storms, air, and earth, has been recognized as the chief deity of the Ancient Sumerians, claiming the role from An. It's not known to historians why this was so, but this trend seems to have continued with, for example, the Greeks, where Zeus became the dominant god as opposed to more chthonic deities that came before him (and lest we forget, Zeus also commanded the storms). Aside from separating An and Ki upon his birth and making the earth habitable for humans, Enlil also regularly helps out the humans in many ways—he was, for example, the patron god of agriculture, inventing the tools, such as the pickax, for working the fields. During the great deluge, he rewarded the surviving human, Ziusudra, with immortality and a place for him and his wife to dwell among the gods. However, despite Enlil's major role in the pantheon, he was not exempt from punishment if he were to commit an atrocious act, as we shall soon see.

Enki was the son of An and the ruler of the Abzu. He was also worshiped as the god of mischief, wisdom, knowledge, crafts, and creation. His role as the god of water seems to have come at the expense of Nammu, the primordial waters' goddess. There were numerous myths and stories recorded about or including Enki. His position as the god of wisdom placed him as the deity that would put Enlil's commands into practical use. Normally, Enlil would issue a decree that would be laconic or vague in nature, and Enki would take care of the finer details.

Ninhursag, the mother goddess of the earth and the mountains, was probably one of the most important deities in Ancient Sumer, almost rivaling the other three and often even placed higher than Enki in official and unofficial documents of the time. She is oftentimes conflated with the earth goddess Ki, and has accrued many names throughout Sumerian history: Ninmah, Nintu, Mamma, Mami, and Aruru. She served as both a fertility goddess and a tutelary deity of the seven major gods, and rulers of Sumer would often state that they were "nourished by her milk." Ninhursag was the mother of all beings, the exalted lady, and the birth-giver.

These four deities were somewhat higher up among the original seven. The remaining three are Nanna (or Sin, in Semitic), the son of Enlil and Ninlil, and his son and daughter, Utu and Inanna (Ishtar in Semitic).

Nanna was the moon god, born from non-consensual coitus between Enlil and Ninlil. He was known as the protector of shepherds, though in later periods would himself be exalted as the head deity. Utu was the sun god in charge of enforcing justice and helping those in need. His twin sister, Inanna, was probably the most prominent deity in all of Ancient Sumerian writing. She was the goddess of sex, fertility, love, beauty, desire, combat, war, justice, and political power. Most of the myths describe her as very cunning and, despite enforcing justice much like her brother Utu, she was known for doing numerous acts that were to the chagrin of other gods and decidedly not anywhere near "justice." Her myth was so powerful that each Sumerian ruler, despite the city he dwelled in, would go through the rite of "marrying" Inanna, much like the original myth of her marrying another god-king, Dumuzi.

There are various other gods that do not fall under the main seven whose importance varies depending on what they preside over. Dumuzi, the husband of Inanna, was the god of shepherds, and his sister Geshtinanna the goddess of agriculture and, interestingly, dream interpretation. Ereshkigal was the older sister of Innana and the ruler of Kur, or the underworld. We will touch more on her a bit later. Some other gods and goddesses include Nidaba (goddess of writing and education), Ninlil (consort of Enlil and goddess of wind), Nergal (possibly another ruler of Kur, alongside Ereshkigal), Ningal (goddess of reeds), and Ninurta (god of farming, hunting, law, and scribes). There are, of course, numerous other minor deities that presided over different aspects of the known world. The majority of them either remain unnamed or named but with no clear description of their dominion.

Heaven and the Underworld

The Sumerians envisioned the heavens as domes made of different precious stones. The lowest dome was the home of the stars, and it was, according to legend, made of jasper. The dome directly above it was made of the so-called sagglimut stone. This was the home of what the Semites would call the Igigi, or lesser gods that fall under the Annunaki. Not much is written about them directly by the Sumerians, though, so any detail on them is pure speculation. The final dome was An personified, and this was where the gods dwelled.

No human was allowed to enter the dominion of the gods (with some minor exceptions). Whenever a Sumerian would die, according to mythology, they would go directly to Kur. An interesting concept that is almost unique to the Sumerians is that their underworld isn't necessarily the place of eternal darkness. As the sun sets and gives way to the moon on the surface, it would actually illuminate Kur, essentially bringing "daylight" to it. Within the realm of Ereshkigal, the dead would be judged by the sun god Utu and at times even his father, the moon god Nanna. Those judged righteous would go on to live in bliss for eternity. Those judged unfavorably would suffer for an eternity.

Much like the city-states and the heavens, the underworld was also hierarchical in nature. Its upper echelon was made up of higher deities, like Ereshkigal and her husband Nergal. They would themselves have underlings in the form of certain Annunaki and fallen sky gods. In addition, servile demons known as galla or gallu would see to the lords of Kur's every need, though their primary purpose was to drag unfortunate souls to the underworld. At the bottom of the hierarchy were the humans that wound up there after dying, irrespective of how they got judged upon entry.

Religious Rituals and Practices

Most of the religious rituals were performed in the temple, which was the most important institution in an Ancient Sumerian city-state. Each city had a chief deity that presided over the city and to whom the temple was dedicated. As such, the priests had an active duty to satisfy this god directly, through rituals and celebrations, whereas the laity did so through ritual sacrifice and backing the temple with money or goods. There would be daily tributes in form of fruit, vegetables, meat, water, beer, and wine, with the unavoidable incense burning. Based on the names of some months, we can ascertain certain holidays and celebrations in Sumer, such as "the Month of Barley Eating of Ningirsu," "the Month of Gazelles' Eating," "the Month of the Feast of Shulgi," etc. Naturally, there was a New Year's festival, which probably landed sometime during late spring. Each of these festivals lasted approximately six days or so, laden with feasts, drinking, and exaltation of gods.

An important ritual was the so-called "holy marriage." The ruling Ensi would "marry" the goddess Inanna, who would be represented by a priestess-hierodule selected specifically for that occasion. This ritual was to mirror Inanna's marriage to Dumuzi the shepherd god from the popular myth at the time that included the two deities. This festival most likely took place during the first day of the new year.

An important detail to note is the burial of the nobility. There is good reason to believe that an upper class Ancient Sumerian was not just buried with material riches, like the rulers throughout the ancient world at the time, but was buried with family members. In other words, the ruler was not to go to Kur alone but rather in the company of his relatives. There are some details scattered all over the literary and physical findings that corroborate this, but as of today, it's still not conclusive.

Sumerian Myths

Any Biblical scholar will note the similarities between certain Sumerian myths and events that occur in the Bible, specifically the Old Testament. This, however, cannot be said for the creation myth, as even today we do not have a conclusive version of how Sumerians saw the birth of their universe. The best clue we have is in the Epic of Gilgamesh, and the myth is more or less described in the cosmology section of this chapter. In short, the heavenly god An and earthly goddess Ki (later Ninhursag) came out of the primordial waters Nammu, mated, and gave birth to Enlil, the god of storms. Enlin then separated them, thus separating the heaven and earth. Enki followed, becoming the god of the watery abyss Abzu. Plants and animals, as well as the major geographic locations such as the two important rivers of Mesopotamia, Euphrates and Tigris, were then created. Other gods followed suit, fathered first by An, then by his sons and daughters. Ereshkigal was banished to Kur, becoming its ruler. And these are just the 'Cliff Notes'—numerous other gods and items were created in numerous ways, some still unknown to us even today.

The myth of the creation of man was more or less a basis for all other Middle Eastern cultures at the time. The gods mixed their essence with clay and created the early man. This early man was weak and feeble and would not be able to survive on his own. At some point, the gods decide to flood the world, which would wipe out all mortal men and bring about the time of new, better men. Mortal men were called "black headed ones," a term that described Sumerians directly.

Naturally, the flood myth has direct parallels to the one from the Bible, but surprisingly also to tens, if not hundreds, of similar myths worldwide. Ziusudra, the only survivor of the flood (along with his wife, of course) is almost word-for-word a doppelganger of Noah. Or rather, Noah is his doppelganger, chronologically speaking. Naturally, Ziusudra is given instructions to build an ark to survive the deluge; it starts raining for a week or so, and his boat lands in what is effectively the Sumerian Garden of Eden, an area known as Dilmun. Fun fact: Dilmun was also suspected to be the place where the entire creation of the universe originated, its epicenter, if you will.

Another rather fascinating myth that has its parallels in the Hebrew Bible is the one with allusions to the creation of the woman. In fact, when we look at the myth related to this, an injured Enki gets his organs healed by separate goddesses. The one who heals his rib is called Nin-ti, literally "the lady of the rib," but also "the lady who makes live." The allusions to Eve being made from Adam's rib are all but cast-iron proof of how influential Sumerian myths were to the descendants of Jews.

But these are just some of the myths. Most of the myths we have saved (in various stages of preservation) deal with gods and their machinations. Some of the most notable revolve around Inanna. There's the famous one where she descends into the underworld and, in order to save herself from her sister Ereshkigal's wrath, she frames her unfortunate husband Dumuzi. Another famous Inanna myth is the one where she manages to steal the divine laws, or the Me, from Enki and bring them to earth. When it comes to Enlil, a famous myth involves him raping his consort, Ninlil, and being banished to Kur for a while until he manages to escape, engendering a few other gods in the process. Very few myths contain mortal men in significant roles, and none deal with mortal women in any capacity. But these myths have set a precedent for the myths of nearly every culture that followed—as pure and honorable as these gods could be, they were still human in their behavior, and as such could fail and be punished. This way, the justice they espoused became an absolute truth to the Ancient Sumerians, and they followed it to the letter in order to achieve bliss in the afterlife.

Misconceptions and Modern Pseudoscience

Rather than a regular chapter conclusion, we have to address a dangerous trend in history today. The emergence of pseudohistory and pseudoarcheology in the last two decades or so has done irreparable damage to the scientific community and the Sumerians who, due to their air of intrigue and evidence largely preserved in fragments, are regularly the favorite "target" of pseudohistorians. Authors and media presenters such as Zecharia Sitchin, Erich von Däniken, Giorgio Tsoukalos, David Childress, and others would misrepresent or misinterpret Sumerian terminology and depictions to back up their theory that ancient astronauts manufactured our universe. The most often cited claim is that the term "Annunaki" doesn't mean "princely blood" but rather "those who from the heaven came." Following this, they claim that An was the god of mining and that his tribe had to mine gold for the atmosphere of his home planet, a certain "Nibiru." Naturally, researchers and scholars of ancient cultures challenged these claims successfully, but this particular current of pseudohistory is gaining more prominence with the advent of mass media. This book exists in part to give you the empirical facts about the oldest recorded ancient civilization and to give you proper context and sources to learn about the Sumerians. Remember to always check the sources you're given and to keep an open, skeptical mind to everything.

Chapter 4

The Sumerian Kingdoms Chronology: The List of City-States, Dynasties, and Prominent Rulers

In Chapter 1 we covered the basic timeline of the Sumerian civilization, touching upon a few select details and individuals. Following that, we've discussed the Sumerian people in general, as well as their mythology and belief system. During both of these, we partly touched upon how their city-states function, how they interacted, how they either grew or fell. In this chapter, we will examine the city-states in a more detailed way. We will cover the major and minor states that marked Sumerian history. Following that, we will discuss all of the major reigning dynasties and their most prominent rulers, whatever title they may carry. Throughout the text you will get acquainted with how the Sumerian state rose to prominence, what its ups and downs were, what notable events marked its history, and how it ultimately fell and disappeared from the stage of world history.

Sumerian City-States

To anyone acquainted with the Ancient Greeks, the concept of a city-state is not that foreign. Earlier societies would comprise of a city (made up of an urban, usually fortified, center), adjacent semi-urban areas, and the immediate arable land surrounding it. There are modern parallels to this all over the world—in Europe alone, we have Vatican City, Lichtenstein, Monaco, San Marino, and Malta. In Asia, there's Singapore, and in Oceania there's Nauru. So the concept of a city-state is not a new one to our civilization. But it all started with the Sumerians.

Before we discuss the major cities in Ancient Sumer, we should discuss what made up a city-state back then. A common misconception is that the city-state encompassed only the temple and its grounds, with maybe a few adjacent neighborhoods. However, the territory of a Sumerian city-state could expand well beyond this area, to the point where it made up the percentual majority of the whole state. As stated, each city had a temple dedicated to its guardian deity and would either be governed by an Ensi or a Lugal. Other than temples, the cities contained houses, a palace for the king (which would come later), farms, public squares, avenues, promenades, large gates, and possibly even separate buildings for the schools (the Edubba); irrigation canals permeated the cities, which were separated from each other with demarcation stones. However, the city center was later walled off from its adjacent villages, where farmers could have easier access to arable land.

The temple, also known as the ziggurat, was the most impressive and most essential structure of a city in Ancient Sumer. We will discuss both the ziggurat and other buildings of Sumer in Chapter 6.

The make-up of the city was not aesthetically pleasing, nor did it show any particular structural planning done upfront. Most of the streets were winding, narrow ones that would tangle about, not making a clear grid. The houses were clustered without much order, with both the small and the large ones often nestled together in an unseemly fashion. While most of the nobility and the upper classes, or rather most of the Sumerian citizens of one particular state (an estimated four out of five), lived within the city walls, it was by no means a pleasant experience, not unlike the modern cities of today, or even major cities of the Ancient world like Rome or Athens. It is interesting to note, then, that the Sumerians effectively gave us our first major urban centers. Again, speaking in estimates, a city-state of Sumer could have anywhere between 5000 and 200,000 citizens, so it's not that far off to say that, for instance, Uruk was the largest city in the world at its peak, giving us our first "world record" in largest number of inhabitants living in one clearly marked populated area.

Roughly thirty city-states are known to us today based on archeological and written evidence, all ranked differently in importance, prominence, and overall presence. The most notable ones to modern archeology—and probably the most active centers of civilization at the time—were Eridu, Ur, Uruk, Lagash, Nippur, Larsa, Isin, Bad-tibira, Kish, Shuruppak, Umma, and Girsu. Other cities or villages that were either less relevant or of equal importance but lacking archeological data, include Godin Tepe, Adab or Udab, Akshak, Borsippa, Der, Dilbat, Eshnunna, Gudua, Harbidum, (possibly) Kesh, Kisurra, Kuara, Larak, Marad, Nagar, Sippar, Zabala, and a still unnamed settlement near modern Abu Salabikh. We will only briefly touch upon these.

Eridu

Most historians still argue that Eridu is the world's oldest city, though there are some disputes regarding this that involve the city of Nagar. As far as Eridu is concerned, according to Sumerian myth the city was founded before the great deluge, somewhere around 5400 BC. Its location is close to the mouth of the Euphrates river, near the Persian Gulf. According to some studies, three separate ecosystems of human activity formed the city: the irrigation-based agriculture system of Samarra culture, the fisher-hunter culture of the Marsh Arab ancestors, and the nomadic herders of Semitic descent. It rose to prominence in the early Ubaid period, with an estimated 4000 people inhabiting it. However, by the end of the 2nd millennium BC, it was all but abandoned, finally falling into ruin at around 6th century BC.

Eridu's first primary deity was probably female, later identified with the goddess of Earth Ninhursag. Following this, Eridu would be host to a different god, Enki, through the ritual of holy marriage of the gods. The major temple, and the city's most noteworthy landmark, is Enki's temple, known as E-Abzu, or the House of the Aquifer. It would be later known as E-Engur, or House of the Waters. Traces of fishbones and other marine life suggest that Enki's cult was strong even in the city's later history. Aside from this temple, the remains of an unfinished ziggurat dedicated to Amar-Sin of the Third Dynasty of Ur were uncovered, as well as potential traces of a massive temple.

Uruk

The city famous for Gilgamesh, its numerous ruling dynasties, and a canal system that earned it the nickname "Venice of the desert," Uruk was definitely one of the most important centers of Ancient Sumer and was probably the biggest city in the world at its peak. Uruk was located East of the Euphrates river, and its history would suggest that it came into existence after a merging of two districts, the Eanna district and the Kullaba, or Anu, district. Of the two, the Kullaba district is older and roughly coincides with the date the Eridu was founded, making the district antediluvian and thus one of the oldest cities of Ancient Sumer. Not much has been saved in this district save for a ziggurat dedicated to An and a few more temples and buildings, notably the White temple, the predecessor to the ziggurats. The Eanna district is far better preserved, with an entire list of buildings, including houses, temples, halls, a public bath, a few courts, etc. It is in this district that we see the first forms of cuneiform emerge, making this the birthplace of writing.

Upon the district merger, the city started to flourish. Its agricultural surplus and a rich irrigation system made it a proper metropolis, and it proceeded to expand and gain prominence in the Ancient Sumer as early as the Ubaid period. However, throughout most of its later history, the city will be under direct control of Ur, another city-state. Sometime during this era, the massive wall, over five miles long, was erected around the city; this act was attributed to Gilgamesh. One of the Sumerian rulers, Ur-Nammu, planned on building a massive ziggurat in Uruk during the Sumerian revival period, as part of a major city overhaul. After the fall of Ur, Uruk remained largely irrelevant until it was claimed by Neo-Assyrians and Neo-Babylonians around the middle of the 8th century BC. During this time, it regained a lot of its former splendor, but its Sumerian populace was largely integrated into other societies by this point.

Uruk is known for being a home to two major deities: An and Inanna. Both had major temples and powerful cults that had been in practice since before the flood. Inanna in particular seems to have been the city's favorite, boasting several temples and sanctuaries, one of which is still not located. A number of artifacts were located in the city, including figurines, mosaics, vases, statues, assorted pottery, and more. The most famous of these is the Mask of Warka, a representation of a female face (probably Inanna's) that earned the title of the "Sumerian Mona Lisa."

Ur

Much of Sumerian history is linked to this grand city. Due to its position on the Persian Gulf, near modern-day Tell el-Muqayyar, it was a large and busy port with many travel-only canals. Thanks to the myriad of documents saved, as well as the royal tombs uncovered, we can assess that Ur was a wealthy city, inhabited by priests, doctors, scribes, teachers, artisans, farmers, and slaves. It boasted a number of prominent rulers such as Ur-Nammu and Shulgi, members of the famous Third Dynasty of Ur, the last (largely) Sumerian dynasty to dominate the area. The period itself was known as the Sumerian revival, or Sumerian Renaissance, as evidenced by the numerous restoration and construction projects and expansion of art and literature, as well as the codification of law in the form of The Code of Ur-Nammu. It was during this time that the famous Ziggurat of Ur was built, the most distinguishing feature of the city.

The city itself was agricultural in nature at first, with major hunting and fishing cultures present. In terms of patron deity, Ur worshipped the moon god Nanna. In fact, the name of the city comes from the name of this deity. His temple is located within the Ziggurat of Ur and bears the name E-Kishnugal. The city itself had a population of approximately 65,000 people, and it fell under non-Sumerian rule in the mid-1900s BC with the Amorite conquest. However, it retained its prominence until it was abandoned at about 500 BC.

Lagash

Lagash was a big center of art and trade within Sumer. As an independent state, it saw successes under two primary dynasties, the first bearing rulers such as Eannatum, the ruler of the first empire of the Ancient world, and Urukagina, known for his many social reforms. The second dynasty, which came into prominence after the Sargonic period of Akkadian rule, gave prominence to kings such as Ur-Baba and Gudea, during whose time trade with many far-away lands took place and art flourished. Even after its fall to the Third Dynasty of Ur, Lagash remained a crucial strategic and cultural site. However, it wasn't necessarily the center of political power at all times during its history; another city, Girsu, served as the capital of the Lagash kingdom for a while, and most religious services took place there rather than in Lagash proper. Both cities remained largely inhabited until about 200 BC, well after the last Sumerians were integrated into neighboring cultures.

The patron deity of Lagash was Ningirsu, a different name for Ninurta, the god of barley. Ningirsu literally translates to "lord of Girsu," showing how important the city was to Lagash. The main temple of Lagash, dedicated to Ningirsu, was called E-Ninnu.

Nippur

Out of all the major city-states of Sumer, Nippur was the only one that never enjoyed political dominance, or even political prominence. It was viewed as a sacred city to the entirety of the Ancient Sumerian civilization, and controlling it was crucial.

The city's patron deity was the leader of the Sumerian pantheon, Enlil. Its temple was known as Ekur, a name that literally translates to "mountain house" and represents the most sacred building in all of Sumer as the assembly site of the gods. This temple was restored by Akkadian conquerors in the Sargonic era, thus making it a far-reaching multicultural religious site. Further restorations were done during the Third Dynasty of Ur, which included rebuilding temples, walls, and shrines. The oldest known map in the world is that of a section of Nippur, walled off from the rest of the city proper.

Nippur was an important site of religious rites and rituals. Sumerian rulers from both sides of the Sargonic era continued engaging in intermittent ceremonies at the famous Enlil shrine, all the way to the last Sumerian-born ruler Ibbi-Sin.

Map of Nippur circa 1400 BC.[iv]

Larsa

Larsa, despite being an already existing site as early as the time of Eannatum's reign, never really rose to prominence under Sumerian rulers and was largely a dependent city-state until the Amorite Dynasty of Larsa was formed sometime during the last years of the Third Dynasty of Ur. Its most famous ruler was the very last, Rim-Sin I, and under his reign some ten to fifteen cities were under Larsa's direct control. While this isn't a large stretch of territory, Rim-Sin I's Larsa underwent a large number of agricultural and architectural changes. Rim-Sin I fell in battle against Hammurabi in 1699 BC, from which point Babylonians took full control of the city.

As stated, Larsa at its peak was an Amorite-led city, but its Sumerian roots are well recognized. Its patron deity was the sun god Utu, and his cult was practiced there. His temple was named E-Babbar, and it shared this name with the temple dedicated to the same god in Sippar. Interestingly, both cities are antediluvian, i.e., founded before the mythical flood.

Kish

Kish is widely known to be the first city to have post-flood kings. Thus we have the earliest Sumerian ruling dynasty with rulers confirmed to have existed beyond myth and legend, the First Dynasty of Kish. The first twelve kings that are listed in the famous Sumerian Kings' List are not known to archeology, and even after and including the thirteenth ruler, Etana (regarded as the actual founder and first king of Kish), the following eight rulers cannot be verified by anything other than written myths. Enmebaragesi, the twenty-second king on the list, is the first ruler known from archeological sources and is also one of the most well-known of kings of Kish next to his son, Aga. Two more influential rulers are worth mentioning. The first is the progenitor of the Third Dynasty of Kish, as well as the only woman in the king's list, Kug-Bau, later worshipped as a goddess. The second is Ur-Zababa of the Fourth Dynasty of Kish, whose cupbearer will later become Sargon the Great, conqueror of Sumer and ruler of Akkad.

Kish was extremely important in terms of political significance. Ancient Sumerian kings would often take up the title "king of Kish" to add to their legitimacy as monarchs of all lands, a tradition which even Sargon of Akkad continued after conquering the city. During the state's peak, Kish's ruler would serve as the mediator in the conflict between Lagash and Umma, merely adding to the importance of the city. The patron deity of Kish was Ninhursag, the Earth goddess. In Akkadian times, one of the two titular deities to take over patronage in Kish was none other than Inanna.

Umma

Not much is known of early Umma, however the city was definitely significant to Ancient Sumerians, to the point that it was mentioned in myths. None of its rulers gained any prominence in terms of conquest, and the most famous historical records tell of a famous frontier dispute with Lagash, which Mesilim of Kish mediated. Umma was always under vassalage of more powerful city-states, like Ur. During the

Third Dynasty of Ur, Umma saw a cultural expansion and became a major provincial center. The earliest known calendar issued by king Shulgi was crafted in this city, and served as the basis of calendars to other Mesopotamian and Middle Eastern lands.

The patron deity of Umma was a minor war god Shara, and his temple was named Emah, lending more credence to how lower the city-state is placed compared to others. However, judging by the tens of thousands of recorded cuneiform documents of administrative nature, we can safely assume that life in Umma was anything but mundane, and that the city-state played a more principal role than originally assumed.

Shuruppak

Another in the list of antediluvian city-states, Shuruppak was predominantly known for its massive storages of grain, with more silos than any other Sumerian city at the time. Not many rulers of this city are known to history (a few are mentioned in myths and poetry, but no substantial archeological evidence of their reign was found), and it quickly fell out of prominence sometime in the late 2000s BC, later briefly mentioned as an area dominated by the Isin Dynasty. The city was, in fact, destroyed by a fire which helped preserve most of its clay tablets and mud brick buildings. Aside from grain storage and distribution, Shuruppak is known for some metallurgy, with arsenical copper objects found dating as far as 4000 BC.

With its linkage to grain storage, it's no wonder Shuruppak's principle deity was Ninlil, the goddess of air and grain. Her temple was called E-Dimgalanna.

Bad-tibira

The last in the line of antediluvian city-states, Bad-tibira, much like Umma, didn't hold a lot of political power independently. According to legend, Bad-tibira was the second city to have kings, right after Eridu. Three rulers are mentioned here, the most notable one being

Dumuzi the Shepherd, later deified. None of these rulers are known to recorded history, however. What is known from scant archeological data is that, at some point, Aman-Sin of the Third Dynasty of Ur held power in the city, and that the later rulers of Isin and Larsa respectively claimed dominion over it.

Bad-tibira had two principal deities, the aforementioned Dumuzi and the goddess Inanna, and their temple was called E-Mush. Rulers who held power over Bad-tibira would be styled as Lugal E-Mush locally. It is likely that the practice of "marrying" Inanna came from Bad-tibira based on all of this.

Isin

Isin existed for as long as most post-flood cities but never rose to prominence until the fall of the Third Dynasty of Ur and the effective end of the Sumerian empire. Its first and most prominent ruler, Ishbi-Era, relocated the capital from Ur to Isin, then defeated the last ruler of Ur, Ibbi-Sin, whom he previously served. The city flourished under the so-called First Dynasty of Isin, capturing most major cities such as Ur, Nippur, and Uruk. However, due to infighting and powerful attacks from neighboring Larsa, Isin was slowly declining, until it ultimately succumbed to Rim-Sin I.

The patron goddess of Isin seems to have been Bau, the consort of Ninurta. However, the kings of Isin largely continued the traditions that included the worship of other gods, like Inanna.

Other Cities

While not as considerable as the city-states listed above, the remaining Sumerian settlements were nonetheless active and played vital roles in ancient history. Godin Tepe, for instance, is archeologically the second city to be permanently settled after Eridu, and its position might indicate that it was a significant trading center for early Mesopotamians. Adab had its fair share of outside rulers, both Sumerian and Akkadian, and various artifacts were excavated at the site of this ancient city, including a male bust supposedly of its most well-known king Lugal-Anne-Mundu. Unlike Abad, whose sole king is the only one known to us via the Sumerian Kings' List, Akshak boasted six kings before ultimately falling to Kish. Borsippa, while minor compared to its larger counterparts, evidently played a vital role among Sumerians, having been built on both sides of a lake southwest of Babylon and boasting a large ziggurat that probably served as the inspiration for the Tower of Babel. Der is a city whose archeological site is, unfortunately, in such a bad shape that there's no practical point in excavating it, but it seems to have been frequently mentioned in early Sumerian and later Akkadian and Babylonian documents, primarily in how it was destroyed or sacked.

A smaller city, Kisurra served as a center of commerce and trade from Early Dynastic period all the way to Early Babylonian domain of Sumer, showing steady decline at the time of Hammurabi. Kuara, on the other hand, was essential in establishing a few cultural and religious elements that would come to dominate Sumerian and other, later cultures. The legendary third king of Uruk, Dumuzi the Fisherman, was supposedly born here, as was Marduk, the son of Enki, whose cult was initiated here and was widespread. The city's patron deity, on the other hand, was Nergal. Little is known of its written history, though, apart from a few details regarding its occupation.

Marad, in a similar vein to Kuara, is best known for its religious background and its occupation by other states. It boasted a ziggurat, Eigikalama, that was dedicated both to the god Ninurta and the local deity Lugalmarada (his name literally meaning "king of Marad"), erected by one of Naram-Sin's progeny. Nagar, later known as Tell Brak, was best known for expanding from a minor settlement into one of the biggest cities in the ancient world. Though not originally Sumerian, Nagar did have a brief period of Sumerian, or rather non-Semitic, rulers. Its dominion was passed from empire to empire throughout its long existence during Ancient times.

As mentioned before, Sippar, like Larsa, was a place that worshiped the sun god, either Sumerian or Akkadian, and it had a temple with the same name dedicated to him as the one in Larsa. Despite numerous documents uncovered in Sippar, not much is really known about this city. Similarly, not much is known of Zabala, a city located in the Dhi Qar governorate of Iraq. Throughout what little is known of Zabala's history, it has been under direct control by other major cities (Lagash, Ur, Larsa) or other major cultures, such as the Akkadians. They worshiped Inanna, with her temple later built by Hammurabi in the city.

The remaining cities, like Dilbat, Harbidum, and Eshnunna, are rather small and do not play central roles in Sumerian society at large, though it's noteworthy to point out that Eshnunna was at the very edge of the Sumerian empire but nonetheless maintained a heavily Sumerian-influenced culture. Larak is a city that apparently played a major role in Sumerian life, but not much is really known of it to say what that role was. The city known as Kesh has not been located yet, as some archeologists deem it only to be an alternative way of saying or spelling Kish, and the site near Abu Salabikh has so few records that not even its name is known to us. Nevertheless, each one of these cities had their temples, houses, areas, and canals, and based on what information we do have on them, they were still a part of Sumerian everyday life.

Sumerian Dynasties

Ancient Sumer is known to have the first recorded ruling dynasties in the ancient world, largely assisted by the Sumerian Kings' List, compiled during the Third Dynasty of Ur in several different copies. However, before we delve into the dynasties themselves, it is important to note that there are rulers not listed in this document, and that the ones who "made the cut" are not necessarily historical people that actually lived and that they might as well be mythological. The timelines themselves will be largely omitted, considering that the

Sumerian sexagesimal system is difficult to convert to modern-day numbers with any accuracy, wherein even some rulers known to us via archeological data are marked to have ruled over several centuries, which is impossible biologically.

The Early Dynastic Period – Antediluvians, City-state rulers

The so-called Early Dynastic Period lasted from about 2900 BC to about 2350 BC, although the dates differ. More generally, it's divided into Early Dynastic I, Early Dynastic II, and Early Dynastic IIIa and IIIb, but this isn't a historical but rather an archeological division. Generally speaking, it's the period that ranges from the first-known rulers to the rise of the Akkadian empire. The dynasties and the rulers that comprised them are as follows:

1. Antediluvian rulers. Most of them are legendary, and the list is as follows: Alulim, Alalngar, En-men-lu-ana, En-men-gal-ana, Dumuzid, the Shepherd, En-sipad-zid-ana, En-men-dur-ana, and Ubara-Tutu. As stated, most of these are legendary and no historical record exists of them ruling over the region.

2. The First Dynasty of Kish. This is the dynasty where we find the first archeological evidence of some rulers. The list is long, and it includes: Jushur, Kullassina-Bel, Nangishlishma, En-Tarah-Ana, Babum, Puannum, Kalibum, Kalumum, Zuqaqip, Atab (or A-Ba), Mashda, Arwium, Etana, Balih, En-Me-Nuna, Melem-Kish, Barsal-Nuna, Zamug, Tizqar, Ilku, Iltasadum, En-Me-Barage-Si, and Aga of Kish. Some of these rulers bear Akkadian names, and out of all of them, the earliest written contemporary proof of one's existence we have is that of En-Me-Barage-Si.

3. The First Dynasty of Uruk. A lot of these kings made it into myths and legends and were highly popular among the Sumerians at the time. The list includes: Mesh-Ki-Ang-Gasher

of E-Ana, Enmerkar, Lugalbanda, Dumuzid, Gilgamesh, Ur-Nungal, Udul-Kalama, La-Ba'shum, En-Nun-Tarah-Ana, Mesh-He, Melem-Ana, and Lugal-Kitun.

4. The First Dynasty of Ur. This list includes four rulers: Mesh-Ane-Pada, Mesh-Ki-Ang-Nuna, Elulu, and Balulu.

5. The Dynasty of Awan. This was the first dynasty of Semitic (Elamite) origin to dominate Sumer. There were supposed to be three rulers, but other than the fragment of one's name, none are known to history, so the information on them is scant. But this does give us a good insight that the third millennium BC saw dominance by Elamites at least in a span of three centuries.

6. The Second Dynasty of Kish. Kish reclaims control from the Elamites, and spans eight kings in their second dynasty: Susuda, Dadasig, Mamagal, Kalbum, Tuge, Men-Nuna, Enbi-Ishtar (not a Sumerian name), and Lugalngu.

7. The First Dynasty of Lagash. Neither of the Lagash dynasties are on the Sumerian Kings' List, but there is ample evidence of their existence. In fact, it's the first dynasty to produce a Sumerian emperor. The list includes: Enhengal, Lugal-Sha-Engur or Lugal-Sugur (who was just an Ensi, not a Lugal), Ur-Virte or Ur-Nina, Akurgal, Eannatum, En-Anna-Tum I, Entemena, Enannatum II, Enentarzid, Lugalanda, and Urukagina. Another king not often listed is Ur-Nanshe, the father or Eannatum, who probably came from a non-royal lineage.

8. The Dynasty of Hamazi. Lttle is known of this kingdom, including its location. The king's list only includes one king, Hadanish, but from records we can ascertain that there was at least one more king, Zizi. Hadanish's position on the list would suggest that this kingdom had a great impact on the Sumerians at the time.

9. The Second Dynasty of Uruk. Having defeated Hadanish, the king of Uruk reclaimed control. This dynasty spawned three kings: En-Shag-Kush-Ana, Lugal-Kinishe-Dudu or Lugal-Ure, and Argandea.

10. The Second Dynasty of Ur. Of the three rulers listed, the last remains nameless, and the two preceding him are Nanni and Mesh-Ki-Ang-Nanna II.

11. The Dynasty of Adab. This dynasty birthed a single ruler, Lugal-Ane-Mundu.

12. The Dynasty of Mari. This is the second Semitic dynasty to reign over the Sumerians. It birthed six rulers: Anbu, Anba, Bazi, Zizi or Mari, Limer, and Sharrum-Iter.

13. The Third Dynasty of Kish. The only listed ruler of the first city to reach three dynasties was also the only woman ever listed in the Kings' List, Kug-Bau or Kubaba. She is listed as a "Lugal" or "king" rather than a queen.

14. Dynasty of Akshak. The first dynasty to come from this city gave the Sumerians six rulers: Unzi, Undalulu, Urur, Puzur-Nirah, Ishu-Il, and Shu-Suen of Akshak. Like with many of these lists, some of the rulers down the middle were actually contemporaries of the last ruler of the previous dynasty, in this case, the female king Kug-Bau.

15. The Fourth Dynasty of Kish. Once again, it was the city of Kish that reached the fourth in the line of dynasties before any other. This particular dynasty spawned eight rulers: Puzur-Suen, Ur-Zababa, Zimudar, Usi-Watar, Eshtar-Muti, Ishte-Shamash, Shu-Ilishu (not a Sumerian name), and Nanniya. This was the last time a Sumerian ruler from Kish would have dominion over Sumer.

16. The Third Dynasty of Uruk. This dynasty produced only one powerful ruler, Lugal-Zage-Si. His defeat at the hands of the Akkadians marks the end of the Early Dynastic Period.

The Akkadian Period, or the Sargonic Era

This period marks the first time most of the Sumerian states were under a single ruler who was not of Sumerian descent. This age started with the conquests of its founder, Sargon of Akkad (whose name it bears), arguably the first real emperor to known history in the real sense of the word, and it ended roughly two centuries later, after the Gutian invasion. Three dynasties are noteworthy here, listed below.

17. The Dynasty of Akkad. The most powerful Semitic dynasty to rule over Sumer before it (Sumer) ultimately collapsed under the Babylonians centuries later. The rulers of Akkad are as follows: Sargon of Akkad, Rimush of Akkad, Manishtushu, Naram-Sin of Akkad, Shar-Kali-Sharri, Irgigi, Imi, Nanum, Ilulu, Dudu of Akkad, and Shu-Durul.

18. The Fourth Dynasty of Uruk. This dynasty probably had control over the city in the waning days of the Akkadian empire, and their early rulers were probably contemporaries of both the Dynasty of Akkad and the following Gutian rulers. This list includes: Ur-Ningin, Ur-Nigir, Kuda, Puzur-Ili, and Ur-Utu or Lugal-Melem.

19. The Second Dynasty of Lagash. Much like the first, this dynasty is not listed on the Kings' List. They held control over the city proper and some key locations. During this period, Lagash prospered as a center of art and culture. The rulers include: Lugalushumgal, Puzer-Mama, Ur-Utu, Ur-Mama, Lu-Baba, Lugula, Kaku or Kakug, Ur-Baba, Gudea, Ur-Ningirsu, Pirigme or Ugme, Ur-Gar, and Nammahani.

The Gutian Period

This was the time the mysterious Gutians took control over Sumer. Considering their notable inferiority regarding law, culture, and anything concerning state matters when compared to the Sumerians, their rule was destined to suffer a sharp decline, which actually happened. This was the so-called "Dark Ages of Sumer." Only the later Gutian kings managed to infuse some progress to their realm but were nonetheless exiled by the end of their century-long dominion. This period is marked by one major dynasty, that of the Gutians.

20. The Gutian Dynasty. Two rulers are known not to be on the King's List but who still existed and ruled over the kingdom. One ruler of this dynasty, the second to last known as Si'um, is not verified to be the name missing from the list. The first two rulers of this dynasty, the ones not on the list, are Erridupizir and Imta or Nibia. The remaining rulers include: Inkishush or Inkicuc, Sarlagab or Zarlagab, Shulme, Elulmesh or Elulumesh, Inimabakesh, Igeshaush, Yarlagab, Ibate, Yarla or Yarlangab, Kurum, Apilkin, La-Erabum or Lasirab, Irarum, Ibranum, Hablum, Puzur-Suen (a different one from the same-named King of Kish), Yarlaganda, Si'um or Si'u, and Tirigan. After Tirigan's defeat, the Gutians were no longer a part of Sumerian, or Mesopotamian public life in general.

The Third Dynasty of Ur, or the Sumerian Renaissance

After the defeat of the Gutians, the Sumerians underwent a cultural and social overhaul. This was the time of rebuilding, restructuring, and reclaiming. While the Third Dynasty clearly dominates this period, it's not the one that started it. However, it will be the last proper Sumerian dynasty to have control of the entirety of Ancient Sumer, as its last ruler falls under the state of Isin.

21. The Fifth Dynasty of Uruk. With this dynasty, Uruk will have officially become the only city-state to span five. This would also be the last dynasty of Uruk, and it only spawned one ruler, the one who defeated the Gutians, king Utu-Hengal.
22. The Third Dynasty of Ur. Arguably the most famous dynasty known to archeology, it would also be the last dynasty of Ur, as well as the last Sumerian dynasty to keep the empire together. Many famous and well-revered rulers came from this dynasty, and these are: Ur-Namma or Ur-Nammu, Shulgi, Amar-Suena, Shu-Suen or Shu-Sin, and Ibi-Suen or Ibbi-Sin.

The Isin-Larsa Period

While the Sumerian empire completely fell through with the death of the Third Dynasty of Ur, two independent states held large swathes of land for themselves, including important religious and political centers. While Isin initially thrived, Larsa would eventually expand and claim it under the last ruler of Larsa, Rim-Sin I. Shortly after, the entirety of Ancient Sumer would fall under Hammurabi and his followers, ending the Ancient Sumerians and ushering in the age of Old Babylon.

As the name would suggest, two major dynasties ruled over their respective cities, one being the Sumerian Isin, the other Semitic Larsa.

23. The Dynasty of Isin: this dynasty was started by Ibbi-Suen's military official, Ishbi-Erra. It would go on to spawn numerous rulers and, while officially a Sumerian dynasty, all of them spoke and wrote Akkadian. The list of rulers of Isin is as follows: Ishbi-Erra, Shu-Ilishu, Iddin-Dagan, Ishme-Dagan, Lipit-Eshtar or Lipit-Ishtar, Ur-Ninurta, Bur-Suen, Lipit-Enlil, Erra-Imitti, Enlil-Bani, Zambiya, Iter-Pisha, Ur-Du-Kuga, Suen-Magir, and Damiq-Ilishu.
24. The Dynasty of Larsa: the kings of this city-state were Amorite in origin, making them the last Semitic peoples to reign over Sumer before the Babylonians took over. Their peak was

reached at the age of their last ruler, after which they were defeated by Hammurabi. The rulers of Larsa were: Naplanum, Emisum, Samium, Zabaia, Gungunum, Abisare, Sumuel, Nur-Adad, Sin-Iddinam, Sin-Eribam, Sin-Iqisham, Silli-Adad, Warad-Sin, and Rim Sin I.

Notable Rulers of Sumer

Enmebaragesi of Kish

A ruler from the First Dynasty of Kish, Enmebaragesi was most likely a contemporary of Gilgamesh and is the first ruler whom archeology can verify to have existed at some point in history. Based on myth and written data, he defeated the Elamites and ruled for some time before Gilgamesh defeated him.

Enmerkar of Uruk

Either the son or the grandson of the sun god Utu, Enmerkar was the builder and founder of Uruk. The earliest recorded epic poems deal with his exploits. Other than founding arguably one of the most important cities of Ancient Sumer, he is said to have issued construction of a temple in the city-state of Eridu. Legends claim that he waged successful campaigns against Aratta, both military ones and ones of wit.

Lugalbanda of Uruk

A contemporary of Enmerkar and his successor, Lugalbanda is also better known to myth than history. He is recorded as having been a warrior in Enmerkar's army and fighting the neighboring states, notably Aratta. Myths also see him paired up with the goddess Ninsun. His legends also predate those of Gilgamesh, much like the legends involving Enmerkar.

Gilgamesh of Uruk

Gilgamesh's historicity is still a question of debate, but the mythical figure of this king is now an important and unavoidable part of world culture. No less than five recorded myths exist of Gilgamesh's successes, but in terms of practical, possibly historical events, he might have been the one to rebuild the walls of Uruk and the temple of the goddess Ninlil in Nippur.

Meshanepada of Ur

The founder of the First Dynasty of Ur, Meshanepada was known for his diplomatic ties to the kingdom of Mari and for his dominion over the region. He rebuilt numerous temples, including some at Nippur, where we find written data of his reign. His sons largely continued his tradition of building and managing upkeep at major temples such as the ones in Nippur. Meshanepada also held the coveted title "king of Kish," something many rulers after him will continue to do to assert their case as the kings of the whole of Sumer.

Eannatum of Lagash

A ruler not on the Sumerian King's List, Eannatum was probably the first emperor to claim all of the Sumerian lands, a title still questioned by scholars today. Eannatum conquered most of the known Sumer, including Ur, Nippur, Akshak, Larsa, Uruk, and Kish. Outside of Sumer, he conquered parts of Elam and demanded that Mari pays tribute. These areas were quick to develop revolts and his reign here wasn't as firm as in Sumer.

Eannatum was known for building temples, especially in Lagash, as well as rebuilding entire cities, like Nina. After his victory over the city of Umma, the famous Stele of the Vultures was erected in honor of this triumph.

The Stele of Vultures, a detail, circa 2450 BC.[v] Photographed and uploaded to *https://commons.wikimedia.org* by Eric Gaba.

Urukagina of Lagash

The last ruler of the First Dynasty of Lagash was Urukagina, notable for his legal reforms. Prior to his reign, Lagash was beset by corruption at the state top, with priests and nobles taking advantage of the less-fortunate. Urukagina, in a sense, put draining the swamp into practice and removed all corrupt officials from office, issued city-wide assistance of the poor and needy, and commissioned what would be the first recorded code of laws in human history. He was also somewhat infamous for his laws regarding adultery when committed by a woman, which are reminiscent of how Islamic fundamentalists punish women in contemporary society.

Lugal-Anne-Mundu of Adab

The only recorded king to come from Adab, Lugal-Anne-Mundu is best known from an inscription describing his reign. Evidently, he had conquered vast areas of both Sumerian and Semitic territory, and a time of relative peace ensued, except for a few rebellions. One such rebellion was led by a coalition of thirteen Semitic governors, all of whom were crushed severely.

Kug-Bau of Kish

The only woman on the Kings' List, Kug-Bau ruled over the Sumerians as the only exponent of the Third Dynasty of Kish. The Kings' List mentions that she was an ale wife, both cementing the role of women as providers of ale in Ancient Sumer and, surprisingly, the first instance of a woman not born in nobility reaching the status of a monarch in recorded history. Later cities and people groups would worship Kug-Bau as the goddess Kubaba, with shrines emerging all over in major states.

Ur-Zababa of Kish

This king is known primarily for two major factoids. The first, more plausible, is that he was the grandson of the female king Kug-Bau. The second, which is more legend than fact, is the recounting of his time as king while Sargon was his cupbearer. It is true that the two were contemporaries and that Sargon came from humble background, but the account of what they said to each other is most likely fiction.

Lugal-Zage-Si

Lugal-Zage-Si was the very last Sumerian ruler before Sargon claimed most of Mesopotamia and is the only king of the Third Dynasty of Uruk. He himself briefly held dominion over most of Sumerian cities, reigning from Uruk as his capital. He was the one who defeated Ur-Zababa and claimed Kish as his own.

Sargon of Akkad

Also known as Sargon the Great, this Akkadian ruler is widely accepted as the first modern-day variant of an emperor, having subdued nearly the entirety of Mesopotamia under his rule. Like many before him, he held the title "king of Kish," having served there as the cupbearer to Ur-Zababa. During his time, numerous temples and shrines were rebuilt and it was a period of general blossoming of the Akkadian empire. He had bested Lugal-Zage-Si and effectively ended Sumerian dominion over their own people for the following two hundred plus years.

Gudea of Lagash

The most famous ruler of the Second Dynasty of Lagash, Gudea came from a more humble background, marrying the daughter of the previous ruler. He did not call himself "king" or "Lugal," but rather Ensi. Under his dominion, Lagash flourished culturally and artistically. He maintained control of vast areas that were independent of the slowly-failing Gutian empire. Gudea was known for issuing numerous statues of himself, which still exist today in relatively decent condition. He also issued a series of legal and religious reforms, including the ability for women to own land. Both trade and agriculture flourished under Gudea in Lagash, and his retaining the title of Ensi speak of a ruler who was possibly god-fearing and willing to return his city-state to its old values. Like all other Lagash rulers, he is not on the Sumerian Kings' List.

Gudea of Lagash, circa 2120 BC.[vi]

Utu-Hengal of Uruk

The last king to come from Uruk, and the only member of its Fifth Dynasty, Utu-Hengal is credited as the one who defeated the Gutians and forced them out of Sumer. While he was evidently a skilled general, his reign wasn't a long one, as he was succeeded shortly by Ur-Nammu of Ur. His daughter did marry the first ruler of the Third Dynasty of Ur, thus making king Shulgi his grandson.

Ur-Nammu of Ur

The progenitor of the grand Third Dynasty of Ur, Ur-Nammu was the author of the first proper legal code in our history, much more detailed and to-the-point than that of Urukagina before him. He was also known for both building and rebuilding numerous temples and complexes, and the famous Great Ziggurat of Ur was constructed during this period. Roads, housing, and infrastructure in general were revamped during Ur-Nammu, and the order was restored after decades of Gutian rule. He died on the battlefield and was succeeded by his son Shulgi.

Ur-Nammu of Ur, cylinder impression, circa 2100 BC.[vii]

Shulgi of Ur

Continuing where his father left off, Shulgi finished building the Great Ziggurat of Ur, and his rebuilding of walls, temples, and especially roads did not go unnoticed. His most major achievement seems to be the improvement of the schooling system and the importance he placed in the written word. An interesting fact to note is that Shulgi built what might be the world's first inn.

Ibbi-Sin of Ur

Ibbi-Sin was the last Sumerian ruler over the entire Sumerian area. He was remembered as a weak, ineffective ruler whose actions led to the sacking of Ur and the eventual triumph of the Elamites, as well as the domination of Isin as the new capital of Ancient Sumerians. He was ultimately defeated by his own governor, Ishbi-Erra, probably in cooperation with the Elamite troops. We learn from the Lament for Ur that his capture was a rather pitiable one, and it is unknown when or where he died.

Ishbi-Erra of Isin

The direct "inheritor" of the Sumerian lands, Ishbi-Erra was not generally seen as a member of the Third Dynasty of Ur but rather as a progenitor of his own dynasty. He carried on with the rites and rituals of Sumerian rulers, even though his kingdom largely spoke Akkadian, himself included. He enjoyed numerous military victories over the Elamites and the Amorites, and though he held most major Sumerian cities under direct control, his territory was nowhere near as vast as that of Sumer at its peak, let alone Akkad.

Damiq-Ilishu of Isin

Damiq-Ilishu was the final king of Isin, and the last Sumerian-in-origin-only king to rule over most of Sumerian lands. His age was marked by steady decline, and one after another the cities under Isin's control were falling under Larsa and the Babylonians. He himself was defeated twice, first by Sîn-Muballiṭ of Babylon and then by Rim-Sin I of Larsa. Strangely enough, Damiq-Ilishu became somewhat of a folk hero to the cultures that succeeded Sumer, with the ruler of one following dynasty (Sealand) even naming himself after him.

Rim-Sin I of Larsa

Rim-Sin is notable for being the king of Larsa both at its peak and at its fall. He is also the very last ruler to hold dominion over Sumerian lands before they fell under Hammurabi, whom he lost against. Before his eventual fall under Hammurabi, Rim-Sin I was known to have conquered a few important cities such as Uruk and Isin and to have destroyed Der. He even managed to lead successful raids on Babylon. He was captured after Larsa was sacked and died in captivity.

Conclusion

Upon closer inspection, the situation in the Ancient Near East is not that different to modern-day squabbles for power. The vast variety of different personalities that dominated the area, as well as different cities in general, paints a picture of a complex, politically active, and socially conscious society. Kings and warlords of Sumer were not afraid to use any tactics to their advantage, be it for conquest, maintaining sovereignty, or keeping peace. But all of these periods had their ups and downs, their high and low points, and while most historical details may be lacking or sketchy, we can definitely see the vibrant nature of the Ancient Sumerian cities and their citizens.

Chapter 5

The Everyday Life of Ancient Sumerians: Jobs and Professions, Travel, Housing, Social Life; Psychological and Ethical Make-up

Sumerians have a grandiose history replete with kings, high priests, heroes, and conquest, as well as failure, laments of disastrous events, and political intrigue. However, an endlessly interesting treasure trove of information arises when you bring up the topic of the everyday lives of the people themselves. We can learn this from numerous tablets with different types of inscriptions, most from two major sources. The first would be the myths and legends that give us a glimpse of what a regular day might look like to a Sumerian civilian. The second source is comprised of more practical documents, such as receipts, almanacs, lists of purchases and trades, accounting documents, dictionaries, and even documents written by beginner students. More on this later.

Jobs and Professions

An Ancient Sumerian had a vast array of professions to choose from. Again, we should differentiate between two groups. The first includes the Sumerian upper classes and the second includes their "plebs." Depending on how you were born or what you did during your life in Sumer, you could jump between these two groups.

The high-class Sumerians, for the most part, were either priests, scribes, members of royalty, or minor noblemen. We've talked about the priests in a previous chapter, but we shall touch upon them briefly once more. A priest was probably the most coveted profession. From the high priest or priestess to the lower-ranking priests, any one of them would have a high salary, temple land (and even lands beyond), and social respect from among the laity. Naturally, they would receive rigorous education and be skilled in writing, speaking, singing, and numerous other skills. In fact, the first people to practice medicine were from the priestly class.

If you couldn't get into the temple as an Ancient Sumerian, you could always try becoming a scribe, or dubsar in Sumerian. Scribes were highly-regarded, and considering this was the civilization that literally invented writing this phrase is quite the understatement. Knowing how to put cuneiform on clay was a very sought-after skill because you could be employed as an accountant, trader, or any other profession that required lists and calculations. Writing was taught in Sumerian schools, as we will learn later in the text.

Considering that "nobility" is a self-explanatory class, we will focus on the professions of the second group, that of the ordinary Sumerian folk. When we take a cursory look at the topography of Ancient Mesopotamia, we can correctly attest that Sumerians were primarily an agricultural society. An important argument in favor of this claim is the invention of numerous soil-working tools, such as the pickax. Yet another argument is the importance of the many gods dedicated to the harvest. Aside from agriculture, a Sumerian could attain food by herding cattle, raising fowl, hunting, or fishing. Nearly all of this food was, in one way or another, used as tribute to the gods at the temple. An interesting fact is that beer was considered a sacred drink in Ancient Sumer, to the point that it had its own goddess, Ninkasi.

In terms of craftsmen, we find a wide array of professions. There were sculptors, jewelers, lapidaries, carpenters, smiths, leatherworkers, fullers, basket makers, builders, etc. Based on the works of Ancient Sumerian scribes, these were not sought-after professions, and most children—and their parents—with high aspirations were encouraged to pursue academic or theological professions.

Artists also played a huge role in Sumerian society, particularly in sculpture and music. A sculptor made more than mere figures as, according to Sumerian beliefs, statues of deities represented the gods or goddess themselves. Additionally, ancient sculptors made works of art that depicted everyday activities, such as plowing or couples in love. The same could be said of music. Numerous instruments, of different varieties, have been uncovered or described in literature; most were used by the Sumerians in religious services. But, just as is the case with sculpture, not all music was religious in character or by purpose. There were the Nars, or minstrels, who would play an active role in the Sumerian "social scene," singing songs of heroism or revelry at celebrations outside of the temple.

This dichotomy of religious and non-religious application of art was another "first" for the Sumerian civilization, and it's no different with writing. Not all writing was worship-oriented in nature, as earlier Sumerian scholars assumed. Genre-wise, the Sumerian men of letters wrote myths, epic tales, hymns, lamentations, historiographic documentation (in the loosest sense of the word), both long and short essays, precepts, and proverb collections. Out of these, the only ones likely to be written in the temple and specifically for temple purposes were hymns and lamentations.

This is where we should mention one of the most powerful institutions in Ancient Sumer, and another innovation in terms of world history: the Sumerian school or Edubba. From what we can ascertain, the Edubba was largely secular in nature and dealt with teaching practical skills to its students. The teacher, as well as the head-master, was called an Ummia, or school-father. Conversely, the student was called the school-son, the assistant tutor the big brother, and two particular faculty members were called the man in charge of drawing and the man in charge of Sumerian. The school consisted of two primary groups: the first dealt with the scholarly and "scientific" matters—writing, grammar, Sumerian, mathematics, etc.—and the second with literary and creative matters.

A student of the Edubba would attend it from morning to evening, and the course was rough and often included corporal punishment by caning. It was no easier on the teachers, who had to deal with unruly students for what would today be dubbed minimum wage. This is likely due to the nature of the students themselves. The only children who could afford to attend the Edubba were the offspring of rich parents, and it was freakishly rare for a student to be a girl. An analysis of the behavior of these students and parents actually gives us a pretty good picture of, as the modern proverb states, "the more things change, the more they stay the same." In short, the way the students, the teachers, the parents, the ex-students, and the graduates acted is extremely similar to how they act today in the 21st century. For example, one essay titled "Schooldays," likely written by a graduate, speaks of how he remembers his school days; he is worried that he'll be late and beaten by his teacher, eats his lunch and prepares his homework from the previous school day. Another essay, "The Disputation Between Enkimansi and Girnishag," tells the reader how the teachers dealt with rowdy and unruly students. Furthermore, the third essay dealing with school, "A Scribe and His Perverse Son," speaks of a father telling his son to behave in school and not neglect his studies, pointing out that most other children his age do not have the privilege of education and have to work on the fields or as craftsmen. These essays are written in a less exalted, common speech, making them probably the most honest uncut documents of the time.

Travel

Though Sumerians are regularly credited for inventing the sailboat and perfecting the first wheel, this is still a rather sparse topic, but an interesting one from a historical standpoint. Most of the transportation vehicles were used for such activities as the construction of temples, with the heavy rocks or bricks being carried by sleds pulled by animals, or for pulling wagons, with either two or four wheels, of various food items. And speaking of two wheels, the Sumerians also had chariots, which were heavy and pulled by onagers, a species similar to a wild ass.

The sailboat was the primary means for going overseas to distant territories for imports and possibly conquest. However, it was not the only type of boat a Sumerian would use. Smaller reed boats covered in skin were also used for transport of material goods. Both the smaller basket-shaped boats and the larger, sea-faring sailboats utilized oars or punting poles.

Housing

Your house during Sumerian times would be a dead giveaway of your economic status in the city. An average citizen would have a simple mud-brick house one story high, with a few rooms. On the other hand, a member of the higher class would have a two-story house of at least a dozen rooms. The ground floor of this two-story house would consist of a reception room, a kitchen, a bathroom, and quarters for servants and slaves; there have even been private chapels found within these houses. They were well furnished and bore quality dishes and kitchenware. Beneath a two-story Sumerian house you would normally find a family mausoleum, where family members had their final resting place. However, it was also not uncommon to bury your loved ones in a public graveyard.

Social Life

An Ancient Sumerian, from what we can judge, lived their entire life in the service of the gods. The workdays were hard for any social class, and oftentimes there would be threats of attack from neighboring cities or tribes. But we can conclude that Sumerians weren't averse to entertainment (minstrels and celebrations) or even everyday gossip. The basic unit of the Sumerian society, the family, played an integral, if not the most vital, role in their lives. Family placed higher in importance than friendship or camaraderie. Nevertheless, lifetime friendships were common and well-respected in Sumer, as can be judged by the numerous myths and legends dealing with friendships and companionships of gods and heroes.

Marriage, of course, was an institution that demanded both respect and religious reverence. Normally it was arranged, but it definitely included a romantic element, such as wooing and flirting. These elements are, of course, common to our society today, but they existed well over five millennia ago in the earliest civilization, which is fascinating in its own right.

Psychological and Ethical Make-up of Ancient Sumerians

Scholarly work on Ancient Sumerians largely focuses on their origins, timelines, religion, politics, social lives, and economic aspects, yet some attention should be brought to their potential ethical and psychological make-up, as this gives us an inside look into the mind of an ancient person.

It is here that we must turn our attention to laws and lawmaking. Sumerians were the first civilization to actually write down their legal codes; these served as the basis for Hammurabi's code, among others.

In fact, this commitment to laws stems from Sumerian myths themselves. Enki, the god of wisdom, is credited as coming up with a list of Me's, decrees that go over the laws of every aspect of Sumerian life. These Me's were stolen by Inanna and given to the humans at one point, according to legend. There are at least a hundred Me's, but because of the state of the tablets they were recorded on, we can reasonably discern only some sixty-odd of them. Laws, in general, were so important to the Ancient Sumerian that nearly every ruler of note, such as Urukagina and Ur-Nammu, would start off their recorded self-laudations by noting all the laws they respected and, importantly, how they got their particular city back in order.

Based on this relationship that Sumerians had towards these laws, we can assume that their ethical code wasn't unlike our own. The "black heads" held positive virtues in high regard—they advocated for goodness, truth, law and order, freedom, justice, wisdom and learning, courage, loyalty, mercy and compassion. Naturally, they opposed everything opposite to these. If we look at the social structure of Sumer, we can see these in practice: money and food were distributed to the poor and needy when the time required. Slaves could buy their freedom and were not treated as poorly as slaves in other societies that followed. Schools and the temple were of massive importance and were held in the highest regard by all. In short, the positive traits of human existence earned their prominence and importance in our earliest civilization.

However, there is one arguably negative trait that was also held in high regard by every Sumerian, from the Lugal to the peasant. That trait was superiority over a rival. Without exception, all Sumerian city-states were vying for supremacy over the others. And this one-upmanship wasn't reserved for the ruler alone—high priests would fight for supremacy in much the same way, as would artisans, students, parents. This was so ingrained in the Sumerian mind that we have stories where animals, plants, and other anthropomorphic objects would engage in many of the same contests as humans.

At long last, we should talk about the Sumerians' relationships with the three principal emotions that govern the human actions—love, hate, and fear. In the shortest form possible, love was an integral part of the human psyche in Ancient Sumer. And by "love" we mean love of all kinds: passionate and physical love between a man and a woman, familial love, love for a friend, love for your country (earliest form of patriotism), and divine love (God to human and human to God). In much the same manner, hate was present in nearly all of these categories as well. A Sumerian who loved Kish would, for instance, hate Lagash. A love for one friend would often lead to hatred of their foe. These examples are numerous. Now fear is an interesting segment, as it almost exclusively revolved around life and living. Ancient Sumerians were obsessed about eternal life; the prospect of dying and ending up in Kur was not a pleasant one, so every Sumerian lived with the express fear of dying somewhere in the back of their mind.

Conclusion

It never ceases to amaze scholars how similarly the Ancient Sumerians lived and behaved when compared to our society today. In reading their documents you will come across misbehaving and spoiled children, elitist parents, smug and self-centered rulers, obnoxious nobility, disgruntled teachers, and arguments between people that, if uninterrupted, could have continued onward into eternity. Just observing where they lived and what they used for everyday activities, helps us recognize a particular social archetype and, to an extent, all the behavioral traits linked to it. But it's here where we learn of how complex and lively the Sumerian society really was. Here we get the "unabridged," unpolished version of events, and the relatability that is sometimes badly needed to a culture thousands of years behind us.

Chapter 6
Sumerian Innovations: Architecture and Technology

Considering their status as the oldest known civilization, it's no wonder that Sumerians pioneered quite a few things, and this is also the case with architecture and technology. In terms of practicality, most tools that are still utilized to this day were first created in Sumer, with some of these creations attributed to gods. These engineering feats revolutionized everyday working life, and some of these we've covered in minor detail in previous chapter. But before we move to these technological firsts, it's important to discuss Sumerian architecture, as it has influenced nearly all other cultures in the region.

Sumerian Architecture

Houses

As noted in earlier chapters, everyday Sumerians lived in mud-brick or reed houses. There were no major quarries in Mesopotamia so a typical house would be made of mud or clay, baked in the sun to harden, with wooden doors. These houses were of simple design, many with flat roofs, and the social status of the inhabitant dictated the number of floors; a one-story house would be typical of the lower class and a two-story house of the upper class. In fact, a few rare three-story houses were also found in certain Sumerian cities.

The common design would incorporate a large open courtyard as the center with all of the rooms opening on to it. The only door to the outside would be connected to the street, which effectively shows how deeply the Sumerians valued the distinction between the public and the private life. This house was called an É, and from this term many temple names are derived (E-Abzu or E-Kur, for example; an E-Gal would be the name for the king's temple). A normal house in Sumer would be a little less than a thousand square feet.

Temples

Early Ubaid temples were of simple, rectangular design. Each of the corners faced one of the four rivers that flowed from the mountains into the four regions of the world; a more practical reason for the temple corners facing that way was using them as a makeshift observatory, apt for timekeeping. It's important to note that these early temples would deteriorate over time, and the new ruler would issue the destruction of the temple and its rebuilding, using only the foundations of the old one. Each newly built temple was more elaborate than the last, and scholars can actually study this progression just by observing some of the more preserved temples of Sumer, such as E-Abzu.

The original temples were simple in design, but new building techniques brought about new architectural additions, like niches, buttresses, semi-columns, and even a few cases of an arch or two. While the original rectangle shape was retained, T-shaped temples emerged in the Early Dynastic Period, with additional chambers and rooms at the side of what was the main temple. More lavish temples had barracks, gardens, courtyards, basins, and walls. A specific type of temple was the so-called High temple, which would without fail be located on some elevated ground and serve as the meeting point of men and gods.

Ziggurats

Emerging from the High temple idea, the ziggurats were a uniquely Sumerian invention and can effectively be seen as proto-pyramids. A typical ziggurat would be a terraced structure, with several levels of staircases and platforms built on top of each other. The inside of a ziggurat would normally be just a single space, with no extra rooms. The top of a ziggurat would usually be the temple of a god, hence the reason behind this terraced and staircase design was to bring man closer to the gods.

Ziggurats were made of baked clay and mud and, like the Sumerian house, were one solid structure. Platforms around the stairs would be adorned with plants and trees, as if to symbolize a man-made mountain. Between Sumer, Assyria, and Babylon, a little over twenty-five ziggurats have been uncovered in various forms of deterioration. The importance of the ziggurats was so vast that cultures coming after the Sumerians adopted and adapted them, at times even yielding remarkable results.

The Great Ziggurat of Ur, circa 2100 BC.[viii] Original image by Hardnfast taken in 2005.

Palaces

King's temples, or palaces known as E-Gal, emerged during the Early Dynastic Period, when the king's power would slowly separate from that of the temple. While more of these estates are preserved in younger ancient cultures, such as Assyria and Babylon, there are traces of Sumerian palaces as well. They weren't unlike a regular temple, containing a big courtyard, baths, family mausoleums, chambers for priests and priestesses, and so on. Again, similarly to temples, these palaces were places of religious service, as evidenced by the presence of ceremonial halls and the aforementioned chambers for the priestly class. It's safe to say that an E-gal was the private estate of the ruler in charge of the city, whatever his relation might be with the temple proper, where ceremonies involving Ensis or kings still took place.

Outdoor Planning and Landscaping

Sumerians were the pioneers of urban planning world-wide, and this is true in both the positive and the negative sense of the word. While a Sumerian would be proud of their city's complex layout, with its fortifications, paved roads, and sections divided into "towns" based on their socioeconomic make-up and purpose within the city, by today's standards the layout was rudimentary and rather unflattering. However, we have evidence of structural planning in the form of maps and written data, giving us a picture of a large-scale organized effort of mapping out what the city should look like. Studying Sumerian real estate transactions written in cuneiform, we can ascertain much about how the building was planned, what the value of land was, and how they dealt with population density issues. If we couple this with what we know from archeological data, it's clear that the irregularities in Sumerian city-building were the result of a mix of planning and organic growth. The planning part is noticeable in the city walls, the district around the high temple, and the main street, as well as the harbor with the main canal. District-wise, there were four types of areas: residential, where the regular people lived; commercial, where there were markets, craftsmen, etc.; civic, where public gatherings took place; and mixed use. The high temple was almost always at the center of each city, and everything revolved around it.

Agricultural land outside of the city would be linked to it via canals and roads. Within the city itself you'd have wide processional streets, public through streets, and blind alleys that were largely private in nature. These changed far more frequently than the public roads over time.

Speaking of outdoor planning, it's important to note landscaping as a major part of Sumerian architectural achievements. Empty spaces and vacant lots were reserved for various projects such as gardens and orchards, and irrigation played a big part in maintaining them. In fact,

Sumerian irrigation gave way to the first garden forms, known as Sar in Sumerian. The Sar would measure 144 square cubits and have a perimeter canal for hydration.

Sumerian Technology

Vast and diverse areas of technology, including transportation, tools, war, hunting, agriculture, and brewing, have their origins in Ancient Sumer. We've briefly touched upon the wheel, the pickax, and the different types of land and water vessels; however, that's but the tip of the iceberg. The Sumerian mind was an active, creative one, and this gave birth to numerous technological innovations. When it comes to basic tools, the pickax was in the best of company, as the Sumerians also invented braces, saws, hammers, chisels, nails, bits, hoes, pins, axes, and knives. Most of these were used by everyday people for construction and repairs. War was another "industry" where Sumerians gave the world a whole host of new tools, including lance points, swords and scabbards, arrowheads and quivers, daggers, and armor. In fact, one type of chariot that came out of Sumer was specifically used for raids, as can be seen depicted on mosaics and reliefs, in statues, and in other works of art. More practical tools were also present, such as water skins, horse harnesses, bags, various clothing, footwear (sandals and boot), glue, fishing harpoons, and rings. In terms of raw materials, Ancient Sumer was the first to utilize bronze and leather while already working with materials such as lapis lazuli, bitumen, clay, alabaster, gold, ivory, silver, and carnelian.

But it's the culture where Sumerian inventions really shined. The cuneiform script is by far the earliest writing system, and it was so influential that it became widespread throughout the Ancient Middle East, and was even in use until around the first century BC, a whole five plus millennia after its invention. Mathematics was a major part of the Sumerian schooling system; they singlehandedly birthed arithmetic and geometry, largely for practical uses like measurement and accountancy. We also need to mention the first use of the lunisolar calendar, later to be implemented in cultures both east and west of Mesopotamia.

Food production wasn't necessarily new with Sumerians, but the biggest invention that facilitated it was irrigation, making the best use of the wet riverlands and producing copious amounts of edible grain and fruits. One particular invention that became a Sumerian staple in all cultural aspects was beer. It was, in fact, so important that workers in Uruk were paid in beer for their services.

Conclusion

Sumerian architectural and technological prowess gives us a glimpse into how their culture became dominant in the region for several thousands of years. It took ingenuitive minds to rethink the way to build houses, plan out cities, provide food and water, and build defensive structures in times of war. What it also took was imagination and abstract thought because only that type of mind could produce non-material disciplines such as writing and mathematics, and furthermore apply those in real-life situations. Ancient Sumerians survived and flourished by adapting and evolving every step of the way, and in a sense you can draw a parallel between that and their crowning achievement of architecture: the ziggurat. Every new level of success brought them closer to greatness, with the basics still there yet strong enough to handle more innovation. This view contradicts what the mainstream opinion of Ancient Sumer, that their culture was more primitive and religion-oriented, was for many years. Their technological and construction-based breakthroughs give us a more nuanced, complex picture of the first civilization as people of great ideas and great execution.

Chapter 7
Sumerian Culture: Literature, Art, Music

With writing comes literature. With crafting comes art. With speech comes music. All of these were well and alive in Ancient Sumer. As noted in earlier chapters, Sumerians did most of their daily things in the service of the gods. However, there was definitely a practical, more mundane, and everyday element to everything they did. In other words, the Sumerians were the first culture to separate art and literature from religion and craft masterpieces purely out of a creative need for expression. In this chapter we will focus on this creative side of Ancient Sumerians and examine these three areas more thoroughly.

Literature

A culture that invented writing was logically going to utilize it for aesthetic purposes sooner or later. As stated, hymns and lamentations were definitely a part of religious ceremonies, and it's extremely probable that writing developed as a need to pass these down to new generations of believers. Five lamentations were preserved, most dating from the period marking the decline of the Third Dynasty of Ur. They are all city laments: Lament for Ur, Lament for Sumer and

Ur, Lament for Nippur, Lament for Eridu, and Lament for Uruk. Out of the hymns, some of the best-preserved ones are the Kesh temple hymn and the Hymn to Enlil.

Most of what Sumerians wrote was poetry, or rather some variation of it. Included are the famous long poems about the gods and three major epic cycles. One of the said cycles contains two legends of Enmerkar, whereas the other contains two tales of Lugalbanda, both prominent kings and heroes of Ancient Sumer. The most famous work, however, is the third epic cycle, which includes five stories about Gilgamesh. Out of all the Sumerian literature, Gilgamesh was by far the most influential worldwide, as it has given birth to the genre of epic poetry. The main hero of this cycle, Gilgamesh the king of Uruk, travels the world and performs impressive deeds with his follower and best friend Enkidu. The epic got a rewrite in Old Babylon, as well as other Ancient Middle-Eastern cultures, making it a true cultural touchstone in world literature even back then.

Other types of literary works would include myths and poems about gods and goddesses, with Inanna having the largest number of works written about her. The most famous includes her descent into the underworld and escape by exchanging her husband Dimuzi for her soul. Throughout these myths, rarely is ever any mortal man shown in a positive role, and mortal women make no appearances. And true to the nature of the ancient gods, the gods in these myths are represented with very much human characteristics—they fight, they bicker, they trick one another, they fail their tasks, get punished, and ultimately get saved. No god was immune to this treatment, not even Enlil, the major deity of the Sumerian pantheon.

Proverbs and essays also existed, usually written in forms of collections. An interesting genre of writing involved discussions between two differing sides, like an ancient form of debate. These did not only occur between two human beings but also between animals, inanimate objects, concepts, and ideas. The Ancient Greek philosophers will later perfect these in the form of dialogues.

There's abundant evidence that some form of "creative writing" was a part of regular curriculum in the Edubba. Advanced students were made to remember more complex Sumerian texts and reproduce them by heart, both orally and in writing. In time, students, former students, and even teachers wrote their own texts, further contributing to the overall culture of their respective cities.

The Flood Tablet of the Epic of Gilgamesh, circa 7th Century BC.[ix] Original image by Osama Shukir Muhammed Ami.

Art

An Ancient Sumerian artist would most often be a sculptor. As such, we find plenty of examples of sculptures, reliefs, vases, and various other pottery. However, we also find traces of mosaics and murals, which shows that Sumerians also painted, though not as frequently.

In terms of vases, the Sumerian artist chose a cylindrical vase to represent the Creation of the World, a technique that was soon widespread. A famous example of this would be the Warka vase found in Uruk. This vase was made of alabaster and stands around three feet tall. It was a part of a pair of vases inside of the Temple of Inanna, but the other vase's relief is barely legible due to deterioration. This vase depicts a procession of men taking up agricultural fruits of labor to Inanna, all of this shown in four tiers or registers, moving in a circular continuous fashion from bottom to top.

An interesting piece of art that wasn't originally intended for that purpose is the cylinder seal. It was a small cylindrical object with elements carved on it in reverse. The object would then be rolled onto the clay to form a signature of an official, usually a high priest or a king. These seals have been used since the Ubaid period, and the reason they're so fascinating to Sumerian (and other Ancient Mesopotamian) scholars is because of the detail that went into creating them. The seals would be made of various precious stones, like lapis lazuli, marble, jasper, hematite, chalcedony, agate, steatite, serpentine, and limestone, with gold and silver reserved for the highest of classes.

When it comes to statues, though, a few are noteworthy to mention. Within the temple of the remote city-state of Eshnunna, excavators found twelve statues of mostly men in a praying position, with wide, protruding eyes. The most famous of these was dubbed the Standing Male Worshipper of Tell Asmar (modern-day location where Eshnunna used to be). However, if there ever was a figure of note who contributed most to the art of sculpting, that would be Gudea of Lagash. This ruler commissioned numerous figures of himself, some very lifelike; one particular figurine is of him holding the temple plan, found in Girsu within the Lagash state, which Gudea ruled over. These statues were largely made of diorite and can be as tall as an average human.

While Uruk, Lagash, and Eshnunna provided splendid pieces of art, one that continues to fascinate historians is the so-called Standard of Ur. This small wooden box, with a mosaic of red limestone, lapis lazuli, and shell, is vividly colored and has two "sides" to it, the Peace side and the War side. The War side shows what might be the most accurate depiction available of a Sumerian army during conflict. Consequently, the Peace side shows a banquet, with plentiful food and beverages as well as musicians entertaining guests. It was originally thought to be a standard of some kind, where it got its name, but its true purpose is still unknown.

Other notable works of art include the Warka Mask of Inanna, which we briefly mentioned in one of the earlier chapters, the Limestone bull of Uruk, The Ram in a Thicket, Stele of the Vultures, and the cone mosaic from the Eanna temple. Most of these works are either partially restored or in a slightly decrepit condition, and much like the Warka vase, often came in pairs.

The Peace Scene, The Standard of Ur, circa 2,500 BC.[x] Original image by Osama Shukir Muhammed Amin.

Music

We've spoken a bit about the Nar, or the minstrel, and how much of a prominent role he had in spreading awareness of the myths through song. However, musicians in and of themselves were an inseparable part of the Ancient Sumerian temple. Music played a dual role, both as a religious tool and as a form of artistic expression.

There were three types of instruments that the Sumerians would use, divided into three groups: percussion, wind, and string instruments. Within the percussion group there were various drums, timbrels, and rattles. A typical name for a drum in Sumerian was Ub, with Ub-Tur meaning 'little drum,' Su-Ub 'skin drum,' and Ub-Zabar 'bronze drum.' A Balag would be a huge drum reminiscent of a lyre, with the smaller form, Balag-Di, played by largely women. A-la and Su-A-La would be a large drum suspended on a type of pole. Two more drums that are often mentioned in Sumer are Su Gu-Galu and Lilis. In terms of timbrels, there were two major types: the A-Da-Pa and the Me-Ze and its skin variant Su Me-Ze. Rattles' names would normally be very hard to trace, but the ones we know of were called the Katral and the Nig-Kal-Ga.

Flutes, pipes, and horns constituted the wind instruments of Sumer. The Ti-Gi and Imin-E were prominent flute types of this era, with the latter literally being called "the seven-note," pointing to a potential seven-note scaling system. Among the reed pipes we find the Na, the Er-Šem-Ma, and the Kitmu. The second of the three was likely a single pipe used in processions, with the third probably containing a cap of a horn or gourd. A double pipe was called a Šem, with its name being Giš-Har-Har if it were made of wood or reed. More reed instruments included the Pitu, the Dun-Gi Gu, and the Imbubu. Horn-wise, two particular instruments are mentioned in the Epic of Gilgamesh, the Giš Rim and the Giš E-Ag, likely two parts of the same instrument. A similar type of horn might be the Karan. Typical animal horns had a variety of names: Sim, Si-Im, Si-Mu, Si-Im-Da, Si-Im-

Du. All of these instruments worked on largely the same principle as modern-day wind instruments.

It is with the stringed instruments—the harps, lyres, and lutes—that we must turn our attention to probably the best preserved musical tool from Ancient Sumer: the Lyres or Harps of Ur. Three lyres and one harp were discovered in the city's Royal Cemetery but are all classified as lyres out of convenience. Two of them, the Great Lyre and the Queen's Lyre, are so well ornamented that they're a work of art in and of themselves, displaying golden bull heads with some elements made of mother-of-pearl and lapis lazuli. These lyres were called Al-Gar, and a typical Al-Gar would have a different number of strings depending on the model—it could range from six to eight, with the golden standard being eleven. Harps also varied in size and number of strings, and there were numerous types, such as the Zag-Sal or Al, Miritu and Giš-Miritu, Giš-Mi-Ru, Giš-Sabitu, and many others. Regarding the lutes, the Sumerians played the Pan-Tur and the Sa-Li-Ne-Lu (originally thought to be a wind instrument by scholars).

An interesting question is that of notation and scale. It is evident from Sumerian instruments that a scale was definitely present, probably either a pentatonic or heptatonic one, or in other words a scale of either five or seven major notes. This, however, cannot be verified with any major level of accuracy. The same goes for notation. Cuneiform tablets were found that suggest written music; however, it cannot be defined which note each sign would represent, nor how they were classified.

The silver and golden lyres of Ur, Early Dynastic Period.[xi] Original image by Osama Shukir Muhammed Amin.

Conclusion

Instead of a summary of every artistic, literary, or musical endeavor, it's noteworthy to point out an important detail when it comes to these disciplines in Ancient Sumer. It is true that a good number of sculpted, written, and musical works had the gods and worship of them as the main theme, as well as purpose. But judging by the abundance of material that illustrates everyday life, we can be all but certain that Sumerians literally pioneered art for art's sake. On various sculptures and vases you will see depictions of field work, tributes, singing and dancing, eating and drinking, fighting, and even resting. Ancient scribes would also touch upon more mundane, regular events from people's lives, while musicians enjoyed playing songs and singing during celebrations outside of the temple grounds. This appreciation for the world around them made Ancient Sumerians not only the world's first artists but the world's first creators of relatable masterpieces.

Chapter 8
Sumerian "Foreign Policy": Relations with Other Nations

As powerful and as influential as Sumerians might have been, they were far from being the only people group to inhabit Ancient Mesopotamia. During their five plus millennia of existence, they shared the space with various peoples and nations, and there was a varying degree of interaction between them.

Lands with Unknown or Unconfirmed Locations

Sumerians would often write of lands they considered important for trade, or even noteworthy in myth for one reason or the other. However, modern history cannot point out the locations of these areas with any kind of certainty. The four prominent states that the Sumerians were on good terms with were Aratta, Magan, Meluhha, and Dilmun.

Aratta, at least the one of myth, was a state with numerous good stones and metals, of wise and daring rulers and high priests, and possibly even home to the worship of Inanna. If we take what scant details we can that don't obviously seem legendary or make-believe, we can assume that, had Aratta existed, it would have been heavily influenced by Sumerian culture, from their religious and ruling system to their language and nobility titles. However, despite not knowing the exact location of this city-state, some scientists still speculate where it could have been located, placing it either near the Caspian Sea, modern Iran, or east of it.

Magan is another prominent state whose location remains speculated upon. Most scientists point to Oman as a likely place, with Iran and Pakistan and even Egypt suggested as probable alternatives. Ur and Magan maintained frequent trade, largely one of copper and diorite. As mentioned, the Ancient Sumerian cities didn't have quarries or other sources of solid stone, and the metals they used for tool and art crafting were imported. This import of copper continued until the Gutians took over Ur. When Ur-Nammu reclaimed the city, the trade was reestablished anew.

Meluhha was the other major trade partner of Sumer, usually mentioned together with Magan. Among many things, Meluhha exported carnelian, onions, copper, ivory, and sesame oil. Alongside Magan, they are listed as bringing tributes to both the Sumerian and the Akkadian rulers, this done by way of boats. Unlike Magan's location, the one of Meluhha is far harder to pinpoint. Its people are described in the myths as "black men," so Ethiopia serves as a likely location, but there's not enough direct or even circumstantial evidence to prove this. Another likely candidate would be the Indus Valley civilization, as there is some minor evidence of this culture interacting with those of Asia Minor.

The most "verifiable" of these locations is Dilmun, a region that was most likely situated in modern-day Bahrain and surrounding territory. Dilmun was probably an important trading post for all Near-Eastern cultures, where both imports and exports took place. However, the site might have even been an important religious site, or at least a place of religious significance. The flood myth of Ancient Sumer has their version of Noah, called Ziusudra, settle there for eternity with his wife, making Dilmun a proto-Garden of Eden of sorts. There are no direct archeological findings that confirm this, so this speculation largely comes from how prominent Dilmun is in Sumerian writings. As a region, they traded numerous items with Sumer, including stones, metals, wood, precious metals and pearls, shell and bone inlays, and ivory. It is believed that Dilmun held a monopoly over all trade by the Isin-Larsa period, in the waning years of the Sumerian civilization. While they were influenced by Sumerians, the culture and peoples of Dilmun were most likely Semitic.

Relations with the Other Peoples

Gutians and Hurrians

While little is really known of the Gutians as a race or culture, they were bitter foes of the Mesopotamian cultures. They frequently attacked Sumerians in raids, employing hit and run tactics. The prominent Akkadian empire didn't fare well against them either, as one of the Gutian rulers defeated their last emperor and began a short-lived Gutian dynasty over most of what Akkad held under control at the time. However, if what we know from legend is true about the Gutians and their barbaric way of life, we can safely say that their domain heralded an age of decline and decadence in Mesopotamia, a sort of ancient "Dark Ages." Most independent nations came to the forefront in this period, like Lagash, and the Gutians were soon enough defeated and expelled from the region by Uruk's king Utu-Hengal.

As far as Hurrians go, the Sumerians didn't have a particularly pleasant opinion of them. If language is any indication, "hurum" meant "fool" or "boor" in Sumerian, thus labeling an entire people group as such. However, the Hurrians themselves were far from fools. Based on their history, they never had expansive conquests, and their most prominent city was Urkesh near modern Tell Mozan. Within Urkesh they formed their first kingdom and either collaborated or fought with the neighboring Semitic peoples. It would only be later, long after the Sumerians were already gone, that the Hurrians would form other powerful kingdoms, like Mitanni at around 1500 BC or Urartu during the 900s -1000s AD. It was after this that they were defeated and absorbed by the local Armenian population.

The Semites of Mesopotamia

As important, or non-important, as the non-Semitic people such as the Gutians or the Hurrians were to Sumer, it was the various branches of Semites that interacted with them most frequently, whether in peaceful trade or outright war. Early Elamites and Amorites would often raid Sumerian cities, taking control of cities and establishing powerful kingdoms or empires. Descendants of the Elamites were, in fact, Akkadians, and one of the most prosperous periods in Sumerian as well as Akkadian history was the Sargonic era. The early Semites were heavily influenced by Sumerian culture and art, but based on the events and changes that took place during Sargon's reign, they were well aware of their ethnic background and were proud of it. Most official documents at the time were written bilingually, both in Sumerian and Akkadian, but the second of the two had dominion and was the official language.

Amorites, on the other hand, were the precursors to Babylonians. It was this Semitic offshoot that ultimately crushed the last vestiges of the Sumerian culture under Hammurabi and his descendants. However, much like the Akkadians, the Babylonians took many mythical, cultural, and artistic cues from Sumer. They wrote in the same script, worshiped some of the same deities, and probably were bilingual themselves considering that the Sumerian language remained in liturgical use long after the last Sumerian was gone.

Sargon of Akkad, circa 2300 BC[xii]

Conclusion

As is the case with modern-day nations, the Sumerians' relationship with their immediate neighbors was a complicated one. There was no shortage of bloody battles, coups, hostile takeovers, hostile liberations, submissions, and destructions. However, nearly all of these groups were influenced by the Sumerians in no small way, and considering how geographically distant they were from the prominent Sumerian city-states, that speaks volumes of just how influential the first civilization of the world really was.

Sumerians
Conclusion

This book offers some of the most basic knowledge we have on Ancient Sumerians, alongside a few bits and bobs of interesting nuggets of trivia. However, two things are important to note here.

The first is that the scope of data about Sumer is far greater than this one book can cover. An amazing wealth of findings accumulated from over more than a century of archeological research can be overwhelming to anyone willing to learn more about this fascinating culture and the people who cultivated it. And it is precisely because of this enormous effort by the scholars of Ancient Mesopotamia that we can learn about the oldest civilization on Earth, about their customs, ideas, morals, ethics, behavior during peace and war, about how they went about their everyday lives, what they loved, what they hated, who they feared, who they adored, what they pioneered, what they perfected, who lead them to victories and who was the source of their undoing, about both the mundane and the mythical of the treasure trove of civilizational gold that are the Ancient Sumerians.

The second important thing to note is that while we constantly uncover new and illuminating data about the Sumerians, it's still not enough in the grand scheme of things. Reconstructing a culture even two decades old is an arduous task that involves a lot of research, and a lot of legwork, but doing the same with a culture that spanned several millennia, in a geographical area replete with wars, destruction, reconstruction and ever-shifting climate conditions, is indeed a Herculean task, or Gilgameshan, if we're to stay on the subject. And while Einstein did posit that the only two things that are endless are the universe and human ignorance, thus positing that the overall corpus of human knowledge is small and fragile in comparison, it is the task of our modern civilization to learn as much as we can from our ancestors and trudge onward all the richer for it.

But we're not concluding this book by talking about us. We're concluding it, appropriately, with Sumerians. In a sense, they are more like us than most people care to admit: they had a long and storied history that included both mythological and legendary aspects as well as more secular, down-to-earth events. They single-handedly created many of the tools, physical as well as educational, which we use to this day, and the ones that were created before them were perfected by them. In addition, they birthed some of the most famous and noteworthy rulers of not just the ancient, but our modern world as well, kings and even queens whose legendary exploits in and of themselves constituted innovations and reinventions. Architectural wonders, institutional foundations, even the early democratic thought—all of these first found their home in Sumer. And, as is inevitable, so did corruption, bickering, wars, destruction, and devastation, all areas that were also all but perfected by the "black heads" of Mesopotamia. But amidst all of that innovation, the Sumerians knew how to appreciate aesthetic beauty, utter a learned, written word, and even have fun once in a while. And while they might have been a thorn in the side of their immediate neighbors and bitter enemies, their culture echoed onward within the selfsame enemies for centuries after they were gone.

Ultimately, that's the best way to end this. The Ancient Sumer is no more, but with all of the things they've done and undone listed in this book, they remain immortalized as the first culture to dare and do what we regularly go through every day. This is all best summed-up by the title Samuel Noah Cramer chose for one of his acclaimed works on the subject—'history begins at Sumer.'

Preview of Maya Civilization
A Captivating Guide to Maya History and Maya Mythology

Introduction

You've probably heard of the Maya and their astounding civilization before. You may recognize the famous Maya calendar that apparently predicted a worldwide apocalypse back in 2012. The media were quick to jump on board this mind-boggling prophecy (which we'll debunk later in this book). Newspapers and websites were filled with stories of doomsday that failed to materialize. Lucky for us, we did wake up on December 22, 2012, when the Maya calendar apparently ended.

But what you may not know is how much the Maya legacy is impacting your life today. Do you love to treat yourself to a frothy hot chocolate before bed, or indulge in an after-dinner chocolate treat? Do you love adding a side of fries to your meal? What about tomatoes for your favorite Italian dishes? If you do, you may not be aware that you have the Maya and the Spanish conquistadors to thank, for they introduced these goods to Europe and other continents.

But Maya are far more than just their food. In this captivating guide, you'll discover why Maya have gained such worldwide admiration over the many other civilizations that existed in Mesoamerica at the time. You'll learn how the Maya civilization developed, the major turning points in their 3,000-year-long history, the mysteries surrounding their demise, and some of the unique places where Maya exist to this day.

Oh yes. If you think the Maya are gone, think again. As opposed to popular belief, the Maya are neither extinct, nor quiet. They are six-million strong, according to some sources, most of them living in Guatemala. What's more, in 1994 one of the surviving Maya tribes, the Zapatistas, launched a rebellion in southeast Mexico against global trade and capitalism.

In the first part of this book, we'll first examine the origins of the Maya civilization and the Mesoamerican cultures that may have influenced them. We'll discuss why Maya (out of all the different tribes that existed in the region at the time) have captured the imagination of the West so much. We'll look at how they lived, ate, slept, whom they worshipped, and how they used herbal medicines and hallucinogenic plants to treat the sick.

We'll look at their trading routes and rivalries with another famous Mesoamerican tribe—the Aztecs. We'll look into the decline of the Maya civilization and how their rivalries with the Aztecs aided the victory of the Spanish conquistadors in the 16th century, led by the famous Spaniard Hernán Cortés. We won't forget to mention the heroic efforts of the Maya to fend off the Spaniards, and why they were able to succeed at this task for much longer than the Aztecs. We'll even track down the Maya living today, a population that is still six-million strong and adhere to many of the traditions that their ancestors once held. In among the battle tales and gore of human sacrifice, we'll look at some delicious cocoa recipes, Maya-style, that you can make at home.

After we've learnt all about the Maya origins, their cuisine, and their most notable events to present day, we'll delve into the aspect that's often the reason why so many people have been fascinated by the Maya civilization throughout the ages. We will look at their mythology, cosmology, and the solar calendar that resulted in the infamous doomsday scare back in 2012.

So buckle up and get ready to be transported to the warm and wet plains of the Maya civilization—it will be a journey you'll never forget.

Maya Timeline

The Archaic Period:

- 7000 to 2000 BC

The Preclassic Period:

- Early Preclassic – 2000 to 1000 BC
- Middle Preclassic – 1000 to 300 BC
- Late Preclassic – 300 BC to AD 250

The Classic Period:

- Early Classic – AD 250 to 600
- Late Classic – AD 600 to 900
- Terminal Classic – AD 900 to 1000

The Postclassic Period:

- Early Postclassic – AD 1000 to 1250
- Late Postclassic – AD 1250 to 1521
- The Spanish Invasion – AD 1521

Glossary of Important Maya Terms

- Cacao – the seeds that the Maya used in order to create their delicious cacao drink, also known as "bitter water."
- Cenote – a type of sink-hole that the Maya used to get fresh supplies of water (and to perform ritual sacrifice).
- Conquistadors – the Spanish military leaders who led the conquest of America in the 16th century, including Hernándo Cortés.

- The Dresden Codex – located in a museum in Germany, the Dresden Codex is one of the oldest surviving books from the Americas. It contains 78 pages with important information on rituals, calculations, and the planetary movements of Venus.
- Haab – one of the several Maya calendars (this one measured time in 365-day cycles).
- Hero Twins – the central characters in the Maya creation story and the ancestors of future Maya rulers.
- Huipil – traditional dress for Maya women.
- Maize – the staple food of Maya civilization, an ancient form of corn (the Maize god was one of the most important deities for Maya).
- Mesoamerica – this is what we call the region of the Americas before the arrival of the Spanish fleets and its colonisation in the 15th and 16th centuries.
- Popol Vuh – the story of creation of the world that was passed down from generation to generation (it was recorded by the Quiche Maya who lived in the region of modern day Guatemala).
- Shamanism – an important spiritual practice throughout Mesoamerica (during shamanic trance a shaman would be able to practice divination and healing).
- Stelae – an upright stone slab or column, often used as a gravestone. These structures usually contained commemorative inscriptions.
- Yucatan Peninsula – a region in the southeast of Mexico, where some of the Maya civilization developed, especially in the Postclassic period.

Part 1 – History
Chapter 1: The Origins of the Mesoamerican Civilizations

Maya have captivated the imagination of the West ever since their culture was "discovered" in the 1840s by the American writer and explorer John Lloyd Stephens and the English artist and architect Frederick Catherwood. The latter is best known for his intricate and detailed images of the Maya ruins that he and Stephens later published in their book *Incidents of Travel in Central America*.

But just because the West didn't discover the Maya until the mid-nineteenth century doesn't mean that they lived in obscurity the rest of the time. In fact, their history is rich with fantastical tales and splendour and a diet that people living in other regions at the time could only dream about. The origins of the Maya civilization can be traced all the way back to 7,000 BC.

The Archaic period: 7000 – 2000 BC

People were once hunter-gatherers, living a largely nomadic lifestyle, according to the whims of nature and the sharp-toothed animals all around them. They had to keep moving in order to stay safe and keep up their food supplies. But in 7000 BC a new shift began—the hunter-gatherers who lived in Mesoamerica discovered something that would change their region forever. They began planting crops.

It's not entirely clear why this shift occurred when it did. The changing weather patterns may have had something to do with it—the climate gradually became wetter and warmer, so many of the larger animals that the Mesoamericans relied on for food became extinct. As a result, they had to eat more plants and grains, so eventually they started growing some for themselves. They used many techniques to make their lands more fertile. For example, they discovered that burning trees helped put nitrates into the soil to make it more fertile. (Don't try this at home.)

As a result, these ancient people started having a much more varied diet. We know this thanks to the discoveries by the archaeologists working in the Tehuacan Valley of Mexico, a site that contains the best evidence for human activity in the Archaic time period in Mesoamerica. The locals were able to plant and eat things that we often take for granted today, such as peppers, squash, and avocado. Not to mention early forms of corn, the grain that would become the staple food in Mesoamerica.

Since they were able to grow the food that they needed in order to survive, these ancient people no longer needed to move around as much. They began settling down into small villages, leading to the first known settlements in Mesoamerica. The first evidence of individual burial spots directly under people's homes dates back to 2600 BC. These early settlements included temples and sacred spots for worship, suggesting an early form of a civilization. Temples, worship, and sacrifice remained a prominent theme throughout the Maya history, and we'll cover more of it later.

But the Maya did not evolve in a vacuum. There were many cultures and tribes that existed around them, and each had some influence on their culture, customs, and civilization. We'll examine these, one at a time, as we travel through time to really appreciate the interplay between those cultures and the Maya. Before we go onto learning about how these early settlements evolved into the Maya civilization, let's look at one of the most important tribes that existed in Mesoamerica at the time—the Olmecs.

The Olmecs: 1,200 – 300 BC

No one really knows where the Olmecs came from or where they disappeared to. But their legacy on the Mesoamerican tribes, including the Maya, is huge.

The Olmecs inhabited the area along the Gulf of Mexico, and their impressive stone cities gave way to myths about giants who may have lived in this area at the time. The Olmec craftsmanship was highly sophisticated—there are some impressive sculptures that survive to this day as evidence of their superb skills.

Sometimes ancient history is a bit of guesswork, leaving you to fill in the gaps left out by missing evidence. It's interesting that there's a total lack of battle scenes in the Olmec art—something that most other cultures are quick to display in their monuments and sculptures. The fact that they depict no battle scenes could mean one of two things. Either they did not engage in any war conflict, or they simply didn't feel like showing off about it. You decide.

Until recently, the Olmecs were regarded as the "mother culture" of all the great Mesoamerican civilizations to come, including the Maya and the Aztecs. But more recent sources argue that the Maya actually had a counter-influence on the Olmecs.

When it comes to the Olmec mythology, displayed in their surviving temples and sculptures, there are definite traces of shamanic practice. Many of their sculptures depict a were-jaguar, a core element of shamanism, symbolizing shamanic trance. The Maya saw the jaguar as a transformational animal, who feels at home at night-time, a symbol for the Underworld. The symbolism of shamanistic practice is present in all later Mesoamerican cultures, including the Maya.

The Olmecs may have had an important motif of a twin deity, that may have influenced the mythology of the Maya Hero Twins. The Hero Twins is a way to express the duality that the Maya saw around them—the complementary duality between day and night, life and death, the masculine and the feminine. The Olmec flaming eyebrows, the first corn, and cross bands are all symbols that would later appear in the Maya art, connected to astrology. Ancestor worship was also prevalent in the Olmec tradition, as it was later in the Maya and most Mesoamerican cultures at the time.

Challenge your perceptions—Dwarfism

When studying ancient history and learning about cultures, it's always interesting to find out what light it can shed on the culture that we inhabit today. Sometimes the things that we perceive as true are to do with our cultural upbringing. For example, nowadays we define people who are born with smaller organisms and don't grow much taller than 147cm as having the medical condition of Dwarfism or "short stature." We tend to see this as an abnormality, assuming that people born with this condition would face certain limitations in life.

Well, the Olmec also saw Dwarfism as an abnormality, only not a limiting one. In fact, it was quite the opposite. As the director of the Maya Exploration Center, Dr. Edwin Barnhart explains in his audio-lecture series *Maya To Aztec: Ancient Mesoamerica Revealed* that if you were born with a very small organism in the Olmec or the later Maya culture, you'd be seen as a magical being, touched by the gods. You'd be enjoying all kinds of luxuries, often appearing in the king's court. This may be something to do with their belief that the sky was held up by four dwarves, and so they gave them special treatment.

Check out this book!

Preview of Aztec

A Captivating Guide to Aztec History and the Triple Alliance of Tenochtitlan, Tetzcoco, and Tlacopan

Introduction

Nothing remains of the ancient Mesoamerican civilization who called themselves the Mexica, better known to us as the Aztecs. Nothing except for their remarkable story.

In this book, we discuss their enigmatic origins and how the Aztecs rose from nomadic tribes to the dominant power in Mesoamerica at an astounding speed. You'll wander the streets of their great capital city of Tenochtitlán, known as "the Venice of the New World" among the Spanish Conquistadors, who spread the term all over Europe. You'll discover the full extent of the city's splendour, visiting its many market stalls, smelling fresh chocolate and vanilla pods. You'll indulge in a taste of ripe, hand-picked avocados and freshly baked corn tortillas, as you decipher Náhuatl, the language spoken by the 50,000 merchants who visited Tenochtitlán every day.

You'll probably wonder how this great city, built in the middle of a lake and isolated by two of Mexico's highest mountains, Iztaccihuatl and Popocatepetl, could ever be defeated. From the arrival of the first Spaniards in 1519 to the eventual fall of the Aztec empire, we'll talk you through the major battles that eventually led to its fall. We'll uncover lies and deceptions in the alliance with their neighbouring cities of Tetzcoco and Tlacopan. We'll also look at Aztec legacy on the world today: how Tenochtitlán became the basis for the capital of the New World and evolved into today's Mexico City.

Remember the most interesting stories are peppered with fascinating contrasts and paradoxes. Perhaps this is what makes the Aztecs so interesting. They emulated and idolized the Toltec civilization in everything they did, although there's no archeological evidence to support that the great Toltec civilization even existed. Each year, the Aztecs performed a substantial number of brutal human sacrifices, yet they were also completely devoted to intellectual pursuits, such as mathematics, public speaking, and the arts.

Masters of their own fate, the Aztecs re-wrote their story of origin, burning their history books. This has enmeshed much of their history with mythology and made it difficult to separate myth from fact. Further complications were caused by the Spanish conquistadors and their successors, who wanted to portray themselves in a good light or justify their conquest when writing their accounts of the Aztecs.

Chapter 1 – The Origins of Aztecs: A Tribe Destined for Greatness

On the Mexican flag backdrop of a vertical tricolour of green, white, and red, a fierce eagle sits on top of a cactus plant, wrestling with a snake that it's snatched in its mouth. This is the symbol of the Aztec city of Tenochtitlán and tells the story of how a humble tribe from the North, who called themselves the Mexica, rose to astonishing wealth and power just a few hundred years after finding their 'promised land,' known today as Mexico City.

Let's look at the origins of the Mexica civilization, better known to us by the name of the Aztecs.

Rewriting Aztec history

The story of their origin is obscured by legend. The Aztecs arrived and settled in the Valley of Mexico around the year 1250 AD, and they most likely came from the North. Thanks to a tyrannical move by one of their kings, Itzcoatl, who ruled the Aztec empire from 1427 to 1440, all the books that told the story of Aztec history up to that point were burned.

The son of a slave woman and a nobleman, Itzcoatl quickly rose to power, thanks to his military achievements. He was set for greatness, and, perhaps to erase his heritage of being born to a slave woman, he made earnest efforts to rewrite the history of the Aztecs to create a more palatable version of their origins.

Another book-burning incident took place much later, destroying more crucial information about the Aztecs. It was done to heavily censor the Florentine Codex, a 12-volume work by the Franciscan monk Bernardino de Sahagún. He spent years interviewing the local tribes, learning about the ancient Aztec language of Náhuatl and their many rites and customs. When he returned to Europe in 1585, the Spanish authorities confiscated much of his original material, destroying this valuable resource. The later versions of the Florentine Codex that did get published were most likely heavily censored, erasing many captivating details that would have shed light on the Aztecs and other ancient Mesoamerican cultures.

Because of these unfortunate instances, what we know of the origins of the Aztec civilization are draped in myth, and subject to much speculation by archaeologists and historians.

Aztlán - the cradle of Aztec civilization

Aztlán is a bit like Atlantis, a legendary ancient land that disappeared and has puzzled researchers for years. Even the Aztecs were fascinated with finding the mystical land of Aztlán. Similar to King Arthur's mission to find the Holy Grail, the Aztec ruler Montezuma I gathered his fiercest warriors and most knowledgeable scholars in the 1450s and sent them on a mission to find Aztlán. Apparently, they succeeded, although the maps they drew have not survived, so their success remains debatable. It was said to be located somewhere to the north of Tenochtitlán, and, like the Aztecs' great city, Aztlán too was in the middle of a lake.

While it could be nothing more than Aztec propaganda to depict an idealized version of their origins and to support their claim of rulership, the myth of Aztlán is fascinating. It was incredibly important to the Aztecs too - the term Aztec means "the people of Aztlán." Although the Aztecs called themselves the Mexica, they did regard themselves as the direct descendants of the tribe that used to live in Aztlán.

The myth of Aztlán

When the Spanish arrived in Mexico in the 16th century, they became fascinated by the Aztec culture. They made several attempts to document their origin story, and parts of it were recorded by Diego Duran, a Dominican friar who arrived in the New World in 1540 when he was five years old. A document called *Los Anales de Tlatelolco* (The Annals of Tlatelolco), now held at the National Library of France in Paris, also reveals much about the lost land of Aztlán.

These accounts reveal the fascinating story of Aztlán and the origins of the Aztec civilization. Translated, the word "Aztlán" stands for "the place of white birds" or "the place of herons." According to legend, the Aztec emerged from the hollow earth through a system of caves, along with six other tribes (Acolhua, Chalca, Tepaneca, Tlahuica, Tlaxcalan, and Xochimilca).

A depiction of Chicomoztoc — the place of the seven caves. Source: https://en.wikipedia.org/wiki/Aztl%C3%A1n

The seven tribes wandered the Earth together, sometime between the years of 1100 and 1300. Then the other tribes decided to migrate south while the Aztecs remained in the north. They eventually found their "paradise," called Aztlán. It was a large island in the middle of lake Metztliapan ("the lake of the Moon").

The science of linguistics can help trace the true origins of Aztlán. The Aztec language of Náhuatl comes from the Uto-Aztecan language tree. Robert Bitto explores this further in his podcast *Journey to Aztlán, the Mythical Homeland of the Aztecs*. He explains that several tribes who lived to the north of Mexico spoke a language that belonged to the same language tree. Along with some indigenous tribes from northern Mexico, these include the Hopi, the Pima, and the Utes of Utah, USA. The linguistic connection stretches as far as Idaho and Montana, supporting the claim the Aztecs did come from the north. Scholars agree the most likely location for Aztlán is in the northern or central parts of Mexico.

Considering that Aztlán was as good as paradise, why did the Aztecs decide to leave?

The fall of Aztlán

Some accounts state the Aztecs fled because they were encroached upon by a tyrannical ruling elite that wanted them expelled or enslaved. Once they began to flee, they were pushed further and further south by the Chichimecas, a warlike marauding tribe.

Other accounts state there was a natural disaster of such a magnitude it drove the Aztecs out of the area and forced them to migrate south. Climatic studies conducted in the region support this claim, stating that between the years of 1100 and 1300 a mass migration occurred to the south-west of the modern-day United States. This was most likely because of a lengthy period of drought. The Aztecs left the area around 1200 AD, so this theory is plausible.

After leaving Aztlán, the Aztecs became a nomadic tribe, wandering the plains of northern Mexico, and making their way south for two hundred years. They endured many hardships along the way before they eventually settled on the tiny island in the middle of Lake Texcoco in the Valley of Mexico, where they founded their great city of Tenochtitlán. According to legend, the Aztecs were guided and seen through their hardships by a deity called Huitzilopochtli, the Aztec god of war, the sun, and human sacrifice. He was later the patron god of the city of Tenochtitlán.

But it wasn't a straight journey, and by no means easy either. The Aztecs made several stops along the way, even settling temporarily in some of these areas. At times, some of the Aztecs wanted to remain and began opposing the priests who urged them to keep moving. Battles broke out amidst their own people, as they wandered the land for nearly two hundred years, from hardship to hardship. Until they finally arrived in the Valley of Mexico. But the welcome they received wasn't quite what they'd expected.

Chapter 2 – The Unwelcome Arrival in Mexico Valley

After two hundred years of exile, the Aztec was on a quest to find a new homeland. They had finally reached the Valley of Mexico, where their priests had guided them and instructed them to settle. However, they were not welcomed by the locals, who were wary of foreigners. Their journey had been hard, but life was not about to get any easier for the Aztecs.

They arrived in the Valley of Mexico around the year 1300 AD. The valley was bustling with various tribes and civilizations, most of them rivals. Professor Edwin Barnhart explains what happened to the Aztecs after they arrived in Mexico Valley and before they founded their great capital of Tenochtitlán in chapter 33 of his lecture series *Maya to Aztec: Ancient Mesoamerica Revealed*. According to him, the Aztecs were "outnumbered, outranked, and outclassed," a stark contrast to the bustling civilization the Spaniards found just over 200 years later.

Two of these rival tribes were larger than the rest - the Tepanecs and the Culhuacan. The Tepanecs allowed the Aztecs to settle, granting them Chapultepec or "the grasshopper hill." It was situated on the west shore of Lake Texcoco, now the central park of Mexico City. Their subway system also features icons relating back to this period - one of the stops is depicted as a hill with an ant on it, symbolizing the grasshopper hill.

The Tepanecs were a dominant force in the area, taking over after the Toltec empire fell around 1200 AD. Many cultures around the time, including the Aztecs, went to great lengths to claim themselves as descendants of the ancient Toltec civilization and to emulate their achievements. However, the Toltec civilization may have never existed at all.

Settling in Chapultepec

It wasn't long before the Teponecs grew annoyed with the Aztecs. Less than a year later, they kicked them out. At this point in history, the Aztecs acted like savages. They didn't pay their tributes to the Tepanecs, and were considered uncultured savages.

The Aztecs fled Chapultepec and travelled south. They reached the area controlled by the Culhuacan, who granted the Aztecs a barren land known as Tizapan. It was infertile and impossible to farm. The Aztec diet consisted mainly of lizards and rodents.

But their god Huitzilipochtli was never far from them, at least according to the Aztec priests who provided guidance. They said the Aztecs should take up deeds that honoured the war god and do the 'dirty work' that no one else wanted to do. This helped the Aztecs to develop a sophisticated warrior culture.

This tactic paid off. Twenty years later, the Aztecs had intermarried with the people of Culhuacan and their children were immersed in their culture. After more than two hundred years of unrest, things were finally looking up for the Aztecs, until one fatal day that changed everything.

Sacrifice gone wrong

It's important to understand the meaning of human sacrifice for the Aztecs. They believed sacrifice was a welcome offering to their gods, and many people gladly engaged in acts of self-mutilation. Sacrifice was often a way to get closer to the gods, so when Achicometl, the ruler of Culhuacan, offered his daughter to the Aztecs for marriage in

1323, they thought it would be a better idea to sacrifice her to their gods. In turn, this would make the king's daughter into a goddess.

Except Achicometl did not see it that way. One day, he saw one of the Aztec priests wearing the flayed skin of his daughter during a festival dinner. Far from thanking the Aztecs for their attempt to make his daughter into a deity, he was so horrified he cast them out. Somewhat confused, the Aztecs were forced to wander the Valley of Mexico once more.

The vision of their new home

One day, as they wandered around Lake Texcoco to find their new home, their high priest had a vision. "Our promised land will be marked by an eagle, sat on a cactus, holding a snake in its mouth," he announced, coming out of his trance. The Aztecs didn't have their own land yet, but at least they had a sign of what they were looking for.

The symbol of an eagle sat on a cactus with a snake in its mouth on the flag of Mexico. Source: https://www.tripsavvy.com/the-mexican-flag-1588860

Hopeful, they settled with the Teponecs once again. Having learned their lesson, the Aztecs paid tribute to the Teponecs and fought for them. They added more problems in the valley where several tribes and cultures were already fighting each other. They fought against Culhuacan while searching for the sacred sign that would mark their new home.

Two years later, their priest finally saw the sign. Huitzilipochtli certainly wasn't giving them an easy time - their promised land was in the middle of a lake on a tiny island. Shallow, marshy land made up the island, but the Aztecs followed their god and settled there. In 1325, the Aztecs began to build Tenochtitlán on the island. Little did they know that a hundred years later the Aztecs would dominate the entire region, and this tiny island would become one of the greatest cities that Mesoamerica had ever seen.

Building a city on a lake

The land that the Aztecs found was just a tiny island, surrounded by a lake. They employed a local farming method called *chinampa*. They created artificial islands in the lake by piling up mud and soil in the shallow lake bed. These islands looked like small, rectangular areas where the Aztecs could grow crops. According to Jorge, M et al., these measured at 30 m × 2.5 m and the Aztecs measured these beds in *matl* (one *matl* was equivalent to 1.67 m). First, they marked the limits of the soil bed by using stakes they pushed into the shallow lake bed. Next, they fenced it off in a rectangle, using a lightweight construction material called wattle. They made it by weaving thin branches together and tying them to upright stakes to form a woven lattice.

This was demanding work, but it paid off because the soil was incredibly fertile for planting crops. Although they were still paying tribute to the Tepanecs, in time, they could live on their land autonomously and grow crops. What's more, the area was defensible because it was perched in the middle of a lake and surrounded by water.

Life was still tough for the Aztecs. Jose Luis de Rojas, an anthropologist from the University of Madrid, wrote that "early years were difficult." People lived in huts, and even the temples dedicated to Huitzilopochtli were made of "perishable material." But day-by-day, their territory expanded until in 1325 they named their new city Tenochtitlán.

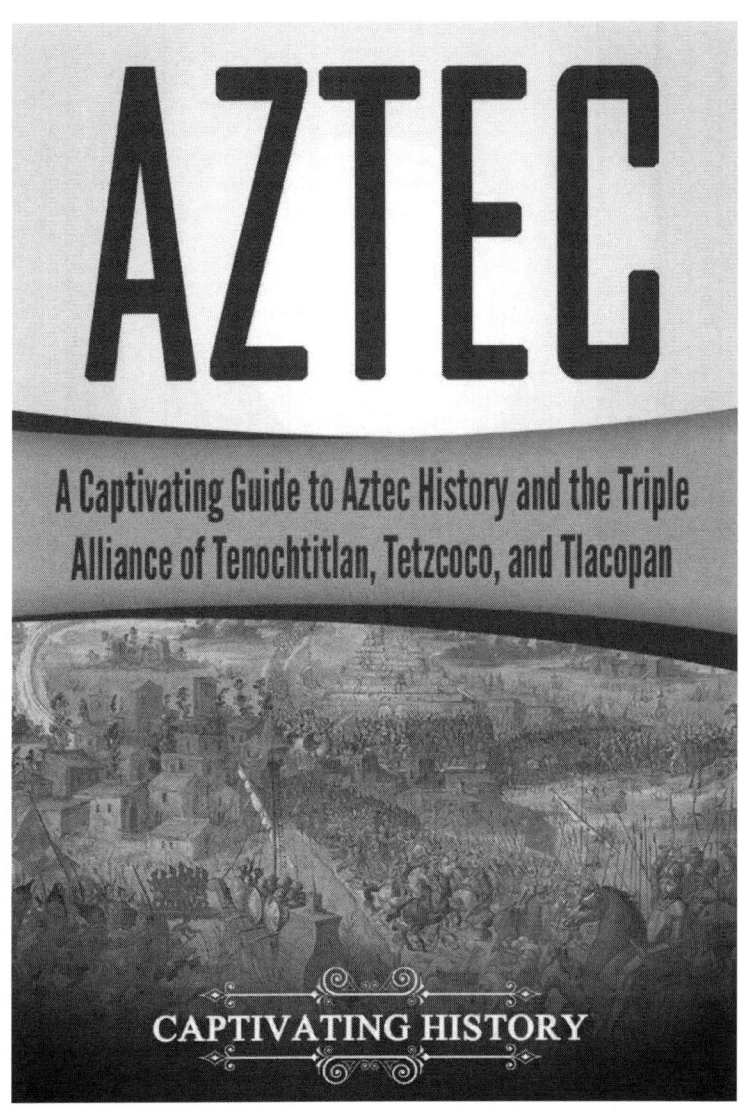

Check out this book!

Bibliography and References

Ancient History Encyclopedia™ (2009). Retrieved on April 13th 2018, from https://www.ancient.eu

Al-Zahery et al. (2011). In Search of the Genetic Footprints of Sumerians: A Survey of Y-Chromosome and mtDNA Variation in the Marsh Arabs of Iraq. *BMC Evolutionary Biology*, 11:288. Retrieved from **http://www.biomedcentral.com/1471-2148/11/288**

Black, J.A., Cunningham, G., Ebeling, J., Flückiger-Hawker, E., Robson, E., Taylor, J., and Zólyomi, G., *The Electronic Text Corpus of Sumerian Literature* (**http://etcsl.orinst.ox.ac.uk**), Second edition, Oxford 1998–2006.

Bodine, W.R. (1994, 1998): The Sumerians. In Hoerth, A.J., Yamauchi, E. M., and Mattingly, G. L. (Eds), *Peoples of the Old Testament World* (pp. 19-42). Ada, MI: Baker Publishing Group

Encyclopaedia Britannica (1981), Retrieved on April 13th 2018, from **https://www.britannica.com/**

Galpin, F. W. (1937): *The Music of the Sumerians and Their Immediate Successors the Babylonians & Assyrians*. London, UK: Cambridge University Press.

Gündüz, M. (2012). The Origin of Sumerians: Re-Evaluation Following Remarkable Excavations at Turkmenistan Gonur Tepe and

Other Sites. *Advances in Anthropology* Vol. 2, No. 4, 221-223, Retrieved from **http://dx.doi.org/10.4236/aa.2012.24024**

History on the Net (November 2000), Retrieved on April 13th 2018, from **https://www.historyonthenet.com/**

Kramer, S. N. (1956): *History Begins at Sumer: Thirty-Nine Firsts in Recorded History*. Philadelphia, PA: University of Pennsylvania Press

Kramer, S. N. (1963): *The Sumerians: Their History, Culture, and Character*. Chicago, ILL & London, UK: The University of Chicago Press

Langdon, S.H. (1928): The Sumerian Revival: The Empire of Ur. In Bury, J.B. , Cook, S.A., and Adcock, F. E. (Eds), *The Cambridge Ancient History* (pp. 435-462). Cambridge, UK: Cambridge University Press

Radau, H. (1902): The Cosmology of the Sumerians. In *The Monist* Vol. 13, No. 1, (pp. 103-113). Oxford, UK: Oxford University Press

Wikipedia (January 15, 2001), Retrieved on April 13th, from https://www.wikipedia.org/

Notes on Images

[i] Based on *Wikipedia* content that has been reviewed, edited, and republished. Original image by *Phirosiberia*. Retrieved from **https://www.ancient.eu** on April 2018 under the following license: *Creative Commons: Attribution-ShareAlike*. This license lets others remix, tweak, and build upon your work even for commercial reasons, as long as they credit and license their new creations under the identical terms.

[ii] Original image by *Xuan Che,* uploaded on December 2005. Retrieved from *https://www.flickr.com* on April 2018 with slight moderation under the following license: *Attribution 2.0 Generic (CC BY 2.0)* You must give appropriate credit, provide a link to the license, and indicate if changes were made. You may do so in any reasonable manner, but not in any way that suggests the licensor endorses you or your use.
Original image uploaded by Osama Shukir Muhammed Amin on 04 February 2015. Retrieved from **https://www.ancient.eu** on April 2018 under the following license: *Creative Commons: Attribution-ShareAlike*. This license lets others remix, tweak, and build upon your work even for commercial reasons, as long as they credit you and license their new creations under the identical terms.

[iii] Original image uploaded by MattF on 26 January 2014. Retrieved from https://commons.wikimedia.org/ on April 2018 with minor modifications under the following license: *Creative Commons CC0 1.0 Universal Public Domain Dedication.* You can copy, modify, distribute and perform the work, even for commercial purposes, all without asking permission.

[iv] Original photo by Hermann Vollrat Hilprecht taken in 1903. Uploaded by AlexRK2 on 30 December 2013. Retrieved from https://commons.wikimedia.org on April 2018 under the following license: *Public Domain*. This item is in the public domain, and can be used, copied, and modified without any restrictions.

[v] Photographed and *u*ploaded by Eric Gaba, username Sting, on July 2005. Retrieved from *https://commons.wikimedia.org* on April 2018 under the following license: *Creative Commons Attribution-Share Alike 3.0 Unporte*. This license lets others remix, tweak, and build upon your work even for commercial reasons, as long as they credit you and license their new creations under the identical terms.

[vi] Photographed and uploaded by Marie-Lan Nguyen, in 2011. Retrieved from https://commons.wikimedia.org on April 2018 under the following license: Public Domain. This item is in the public domain, and can be used, copied, and modified without any restrictions.

[vii] Based on *Wikipedia* content that has been reviewed, edited, and republished. Original image by Donald A. Mackenzie. Retrieved from https://www.ancient.eu/ on April 2018 under the following license: *Public Domain*. This item is in the public domain, and can be used, copied, and modified without any restrictions.

[viii] Based on *Wikipedia* content that has been reviewed, edited, and republished. Original image by Hardnfast taken in 2005. Retrieved from https://www.ancient.eu/ on April 2018 under the following license: *Creative Commons: Attribution-ShareAlike*. This license lets others remix, tweak, and build upon your work even for commercial reasons, as long as they credit you and license their new creations under the identical terms.

[ix] Original image uploaded by Osama Shukir Muhammed Amin on April 2016. Retrieved from https://www.ancient.eu on April 2018 under the following license:Creative Commons: Attribution-NonCommercial-ShareAlike. This license lets others remix, tweak, and build upon your work even for commercial reasons, as long as they credit you and license their new creations under the identical terms.

[x] Original image uploaded by Osama Shukir Muhammed Amin on April 2018. Retrieved from https://www.ancient.eu on April 2018 under the following license:Creative Commons: Attribution-NonCommercial-ShareAlike. This license lets others remix, tweak, and build upon your work even for commercial reasons, as long as they credit you and license their new creations under the identical terms.

[xi] Original image uploaded by Osama Shukir Muhammed Amin on March 2014. Retrieved from https://www.ancient.eu on April 2018 under the following license:Creative Commons: Attribution-NonCommercial-ShareAlike. This license lets others remix, tweak, and build upon your work even for commercial reasons, as long as they credit you and license their new creations under the identical terms.

[xii] Photographed Iraqi Directorate General of Antiquities in the 1960s. Retrieved from https://commons.wikimedia.org on April 2018 under the following license: Public Domain. This item is in the public domain, and can be used, copied, and modified without any restrictions.

Free Bonus from Captivating History (Available for a Limited time)

Hi History Lovers!

Now you have a chance to join our exclusive history list so you can get your first history ebook for free as well as discounts and a potential to get more history books for free! Simply visit the link below to join.

Captivatinghistory.com/ebook

Also, make sure to follow us on:

Twitter: @Captivhistory

Facebook: Captivating History:@captivatinghistory

ABOUT CAPTIVATING HISTORY

A lot of history books just contain dry facts that will eventually bore the reader. That's why Captivating History was created. Now you can enjoy history books that will mesmerize you. But be careful though, hours can fly by, and before you know it; you're up reading way past bedtime.

Get your first history book for free here:
http://www.captivatinghistory.com/ebook

Make sure to follow us on Twitter: @CaptivHistory
and Facebook: www.facebook.com/captivatinghistory so you can get all of our updates!

Printed in Great Britain
by Amazon